Adirondack Trails
Eastern Region

Adirondack
ADK
Mountain Club

Third Edition
Forest Preserve Series (3rd ed.), Volume VI

Editor, David Thomas-Train
Series Editor, Neal S. Burdick

Adirondack Mountain Club, Inc.
Lake George, NY

Cover: Pharaoh Wilderness from Treadway Mt. Photograph by Carl Heilman II
Other photographs by James Appleyard, Nancie Battaglia, Carl Heilman II,
John Kettlewell, Richard Nowicki, B. T. Sullivan, and Jeffrey Trubisz
Maps by Therese S. Brosseau
Design by Ann Hough
First edition 1987. Second edition 1994. Third edition 2008.

 Published by the Adirondack Mountain Club, Inc.
814 Goggins Road, Lake George, NY 12845-4117
www.adk.org

The Adirondack Mountain Club is dedicated to the protection and responsible recreational use of the New York State Forest Preserve and other parks, wild lands, and waters, vital to our members and chapters. The Club, founded in 1922, is a member-directed organization committed to public service and stewardship. ADK employs a balanced approach to outdoor recreation, advocacy, environmental education, and natural resource conservation.

ADK encourages the involvement of all people in its mission and activities; its goal is to be a community that is comfortable, inviting, and accessible.

Library of Congress Cataloging-in-Publication Data

Adirondack trails. Eastern region / editor, David Thomas-Train. -- 3rd ed.
    p. cm. -- (Forest Preserve series (3rd ed.) ; v. 6)
  Rev. ed. of: Guide to Adirondack trails. Eastern region / by Carl Heilman II.
2nd ed. 1994.
  Includes index.
  ISBN-13: 978-1-931951-23-4 (pbk.)
  ISBN-10: 1-931951-23-3 (pbk.)
1. Hiking--New York (State)--Adirondack Park--Guidebooks. 2. Trails--New
York (State)--Adirondack Park--Guidebooks. 3. Adirondack Park (N.Y.)--
Guidebooks. I. Thomas-Train, David, 1951- II. Heilman, Carl, 1954- Guide to
Adirondack trails. Eastern region. III. Adirondack Mountain Club.

  GV199.42.N652A3474 2008
  796.5109747'5--dc22

                              2008024610

ISBN 10: 1-931951-23-3 ISBN 1-931951-07-1 (set)
ISBN 13: 978-1-931951-23-4

Printed in the United States of America
15 14 13 12 11 10 09 08   1 2 3 4 5 6 7 8 9 10

DEDICATION

To Nature's dwindling wilderness: the places and creatures on which so much depends, and those who protect them.

—*David Thomas-Train*

We Welcome Your Comments

Use of information in this book is at the sole discretion and risk of the hiker. ADK, and its authors and editors, makes every effort to keep our guidebooks up-to-date; however, trail conditions are always changing.

In addition to reviewing the material in this book, hikers should assess their ability, physical condition, and preparation, as well as likely weather conditions, before a trip. For more information on preparation, equipment, and how to address emergencies, see the introduction.

If you note a discrepancy in this book or wish to forward a suggestion, we welcome your comments. Please cite book title, year of most recent copyright and printing (see copyright page), trail, page number, and date of your observation. Thanks for your help!

Please address your comments to:
Publications
Adirondack Mountain Club
814 Goggins Road
Lake George, NY 12845-4117
518-668-4447, ext. 23
pubs@adk.org

Emergencies

For in-town or roadside emergencies call 911. For wilderness emergencies, call DEC dispatch at: 518-891-0235 (see p. 29).

Contents

Adirondack Park: Eastern Region

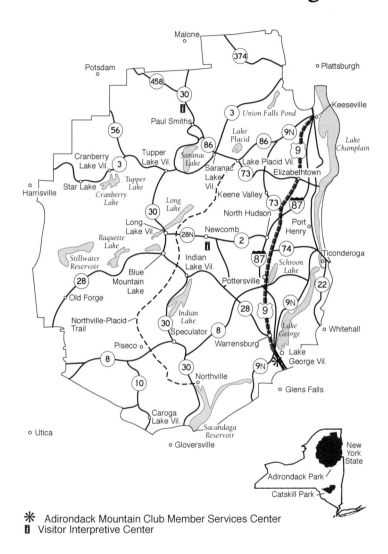

＊ Adirondack Mountain Club Member Services Center

🛈 Visitor Interpretive Center

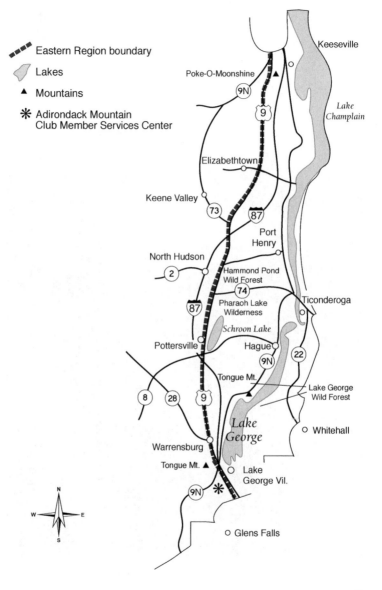

Eastern Region boundary

Lakes

▲ Mountains

✳ Adirondack Mountain
Club Member Services Center

Keeseville

Poke-O-Moonshine ▲

Lake Champlain

9N

9

Elizabethtown

Keene Valley

73   87

Port Henry

North Hudson

2

Hammond Pond Wild Forest

74   Ticonderoga

87

Pharaoh Lake Wilderness

Schroon Lake

Pottersville

Hague

9N   22

Tongue Mt.

Lake George Wild Forest

8   28   9

Lake George

Whitehall

Warrensburg

Tongue Mt. ▲

Lake George Vil.

9N   ✳

Glens Falls

N
W — E
S

Lake George from Record Hill, near Anthony's Nose. CARL HEILMAN II

Preface

Each region of the Adirondacks has its own distinct appeal and the Eastern Region is no exception. Bordered by Lake Champlain on the east, the High Peaks, Hoffman Notch Wilderness, and Schroon Lake on the west, and containing the Lake George area in the south, this region is characterized by rolling mountains and foothills, numerous isolated ponds, and some beautiful lakes. Scenery varies from subtle and serene shoreline views to spectacular vistas from lookouts and mountaintops. Many of the trails in the region lead to or connect bodies of water. So, while walking the trails is enjoyable in itself, hiking the trails with a small ultralight canoe adds a whole new dimension to exploring the eastern Adirondacks.

This third edition of *Adirondack Trails: Eastern Region* is a substantial revision of the second. Not only have there been a number of changes on the trails themselves, but there are also a number of entirely new trails, particularly as parts of new Nature Conservancy preserves.

The format includes the numbering of all trails with coordinates locating the trail on one of the National Geographic *Trails Illustrated Maps*. The maps provide trail locations, lean-to locations, mileage, parking areas, and suggested trail uses.

In addition, there are now descriptions of potential winter uses of each trail for both ski touring and snowshoeing where appropriate. The list of trails includes only those trails either on public lands or those with public right-of-way, to help avoid problems with private land being closed in the future and potential conflicts with private landowners.

The following is slightly adapted from Carl Heilman's Preface to the second edition, since I endorse his views. In rewriting this guide, I have not included most of the many fine bushwhacks in the region. There are no towering high peaks in the eastern region, but there are many fine lookouts and open rock knobs with spectacular views of the High Peaks, Lake Champlain and Vermont, and the rolling hills of the eastern Adirondacks. One of the appeals of these isolated unmarked lookouts is the challenge of exploring the region and finding them on your own. The purpose of this guidebook is to help people safely traverse the marked and maintained trails throughout the region and to introduce people to its beauty, not to stake out every unknown lookout and untracked pond. As pressures continue to mount on the wild regions of the Earth, my hope is that there will always be some uncharted wilderness for the backcountry adventurer.

The Pharaoh Lake Wilderness, one of the two wilderness areas within the scope of this guidebook, sees a lot of use throughout the summer season. Some parts of this region suffer from considerable overuse, while trails a short distance away are seldom used. To help maintain the character of wilderness, consider seeking out the lesser-used trails, or visit some of the other areas in the region. Although there are only two designated Wilderness Areas in the eastern section, some of the trails in the Wild Forest regions are just as isolated, wild, and beautiful as any found in the Adirondack Park. Our use of these sensitive areas determines the quality of every other person's wilderness experience. It is only through our own proper actions (or inactions) that the character of these regions will be maintained for the future.

—David Thomas-Train
Keene Valley, New York
February 2008

Introduction

The Adirondack Mountain Club
Forest Preserve Series

The Forest Preserve Series of guides to Adirondack and Catskill trails covers hiking opportunities on the approximately 2.8 million acres of Forest Preserve (public) land within the Adirondack and Catskill parks. The Adirondack Mountain Club (ADK) published its first guidebook, covering the High Peaks and parts of the Northville–Placid Trail, in 1934. In the early 1980s, coinciding with the decade-long centennial celebration of the enactment of the Forest Preserve legislation in 1885, ADK set out to achieve its goal of completing a series of guides that would cover the two parks. Each guide in this series, listed below, is revised on a regular schedule.

Vol. I: *Adirondack Trails: High Peaks Region*
Vol. II: *Adirondack Trails: Northern Region*
Vol. III: *Adirondack Trails: Central Region*
Vol. IV: *Adirondack Trails: Northville–Placid Trail*
Vol. V: *Adirondack Trails: West-Central Region*
Vol. VI: *Adirondack Trails: Eastern Region*
Vol. VII: *Adirondack Trails: Southern Region*
Vol. VIII: *Catskill Trails*

The public lands that constitute the Forest Preserve are unique among all other wild public lands in the United States because they enjoy constitutional protection against sale or development. The story of this unique protection begins in the 1800s and continues today as groups such as ADK strive to guard it. This responsibility also rests with the public, who are expected not to degrade the Forest Preserve in any way while enjoying its wonders. The Forest Preserve Series of trail guides seeks not only to show hikers, skiers, and snowshoers where to enjoy their activities, but also to offer guidelines whereby users can minimize their impact on the land.

The Adirondacks

The Adirondack region of northern New York is unique in many ways. It contains the only mountains in the eastern United States that are not geologically Appalachian. In the late 1800s it was the first forested area in the nation to benefit from enlightened conservation measures. At roughly the same time it was also the most prestigious resort area in the country. In the twentieth century, the Adirondacks became the only place in the Western Hemisphere to host two winter Olympiads. In the 1970s the region was the first of significant size in the nation to be subjected to comprehensive land use controls. The Adirondack Forest Preserve (see below) is part of the only wild lands preserve in the nation whose fate lies in the hands of the voters of the entire state in which it is located.

Geologically, the Adirondacks are a southern appendage of the Canadian Shield. In the United States the Shield bedrock, which is over one billion years old, mostly lies concealed under younger rock, but it is well exposed in a few regions. Upward doming of the Adirondack mass in the past few million years—a process that is still going on, resulting in the mountains rising a few millimeters every century—is responsible for erosional stripping of the younger rock cover. The stream-carved topography has been extensively modified by the sculpting of glaciers, which, on at least four widely separated occasions during the Ice Age, completely covered the mountains.

Ecologically, the Adirondacks are part of a vegetation transition zone, with the northern, largely coniferous boreal forest (from the Greek god Boreas, owner of the north wind, whose name can be found on a mountain peak and series of ponds in the High Peaks region) and the southern deciduous forest, exemplified by beech-maple stands, intermingling to present a pleasing array of forest tree species. Different vegetation zones are also encountered as one ascends the higher mountains in the Adirondacks; the tops of the highest peaks are truly arctic, with mosses and lichens that are common hundreds of miles to the north.

A rugged and heavily forested region, the Adirondacks were generally not hospitable to Native Americans, who used the region principally for hunting. Remnants of ancient campgrounds have been found in some locations. The native legacy survives principally in place names.

The first European to see the Adirondacks was likely the French explorer Jacques Cartier, who on his first trip up the St. Lawrence River in 1535 stood on top of Mont Royal (now within the city of Montreal) and discerned high ground to the south. Closer looks were had by Samuel de Champlain and Henry Hudson, who came from the north and south, respectively, within a few weeks of each other in 1609.

For the next two centuries the Champlain Valley to the east of the Adirondacks was a battleground. Iroquois, Algonquin, French, British, and eventually American fighters struggled for control over the valley and with it supremacy over the continent. Settlers slowly filled the St. Lawrence Valley to the north, the Mohawk Valley to the south, and somewhat later, the Black River Valley to the west. Meanwhile the vast, rolling forests of the interior slumbered in virtual isolation, disturbed only by an occasional hunter, timber cruiser, or wanderer.

With the coming of the nineteenth century, people discovered the Adirondacks. Virtually unknown as late as the 1830s (the source of the Nile River was located before the source of the Hudson), by 1850 the Adirondacks made New York the leading timber-producing state in the nation. This distinction did not last for long, though, as the supply of timber was quickly brought close to extinction. Meanwhile, mineral resources, particularly iron, were being exploited.

After the Civil War, people began to look toward the Adirondacks for recreation. At the same time, resource conservation and wilderness preservation ideas began to take hold, sometimes conflicting with the newfound recreational interests. Conservation and preservation concepts were given legal standing in 1885, when the New York State legislature created the Adirondack Forest Preserve and directed that "the lands now or hereafter constituting the Forest Preserve shall be forever kept as wild forest lands." This action marked the first time a state government had set aside a significant piece of wilderness for reasons other than its scenic uniqueness.

In 1892, the legislature created the Adirondack State Park, consisting of Adirondack Forest Preserve land plus all privately owned land within a somewhat arbitrary boundary surrounding the Adirondacks, known as the "blue line" because it was drawn in blue on a large state map when it was first established. In 1894, in response to continuing abuses of the Forest Preserve law, the state's voters approved the inclusion of the "forever wild" portion of that law in the constitution of New York State, thus creating the only preserve in the nation that has constitutional protection. Today the Forest Preserve (the lands owned by the people of the State of New York) includes 2.5 million acres within the 6-million-acre Adirondack Park, the largest park in the nation outside of Alaska.

After World War I, tourism gradually took over as the primary industry in the Adirondacks. The growth of the second-home industry spurred implementation of land use plans and an Adirondack Park Agency to manage them. While the plans and the Agency have remained controversial, they indicate the need to address the issues facing the Adirondacks boldly and innovatively.

State Land Units and Classifications

Since 1972, most Forest Preserve lands in the Adirondacks have been classified as either Wilderness, Primitive, or Wild Forest, depending on the size of the unit and the types of use thought to be desirable for that unit. The largest and most remote units are generally Wilderness, with only foot travel permitted and minimum facilities such as lean-tos.

Primitive areas are similar, but with a nonconforming "structure" such as a fire tower, road, or private inholding. Wild Forest areas are generally smaller but potentially more intensively used, with motorized travel or snowmobiles permitted on designated trails. Management of each unit is prescribed in a unit management plan (UMP), which determines what facilities, such as trails or shelters, will be built and maintained as well as any special regulations needed to manage each unit effectively.

Most trails described in this volume are located in the following units:
- **Wilderness Areas:** Hoffman Notch; Pharaoh Lake
- **Primitive Areas:** Hague Brook
- **Wild Forest Areas:** Hammond Pond; Lake George; Wilcox Lake

Using This Guidebook

The trails described in this book are all in the east region of the Adirondacks, which is located in the southeast quadrant of the Adirondack State Park (see pp. 6 and 7, National Geographic *Trails Illustrated Map: Adirondack Park, #743, Lake George/Great Sacandaga*, and *Trails Illustrated Map: Adirondack Park, #742, Lake Placid/High Peaks*) and includes the settlements of Bolton Landing, Corinth, Lake George, Lake Luzerne, Northville, Ticonderoga, and Warrensburg. The private holdings and roads within this area divide the public Forest Preserve lands into separate areas or "units"; users must be aware that there are different regulations governing use of different land units. (See the DEC Web site for details: www.dec.ny.gov.)

Like all the volumes in the ADK Forest Preserve Series of guides to Adirondack and Catskill trails, this book is intended to be both a reference tool for planning trips and a field guide to carry on the trail. All introductory material should be read carefully; it contains important information regarding current camping and hiking regulations as well as numerous suggestions for safe and proper travel by foot in the Adirondacks.

The guide is divided into geographic sections: Northern; Hammond Pond Wild Forest, Crown Point, Moriah; Pharaoh Lake Wilderness, Schroon Lake, Ticonderoga; Northwestern Lake George Wild Forest; Southeastern Lake George Wild Forest. The introduction to each of these sections gives hikers an idea of the opportunities available in that area as well as information on facilities and regulations common to that section. Each section's introduction also provides recommended hikes in the "short," "moderate," and "harder" categories. Many of these recommended hikes incorporate lesser-used trails in an attempt to make hikers aware of the many beautiful and seldom-visited places aside from the most popular hiking, climbing, and camping areas.

Abbreviations and Conventions

In each of the books in the Forest Preserve Series, R and L, with periods omitted, are used for right and left. The R and L banks of a stream are determined by looking downstream. Likewise, the R fork of a stream is on the R when one faces downstream. N, S, E, and W, again without periods, are used for north, south, east, and west. Compass bearings are given in degrees. N is 0 degrees, E is 90 degrees, S is 180 degrees, and W is 270 degrees.

The following abbreviations are used in the text and on the maps:

ADK   Adirondack Mountain Club
APA   Adirondack Park Agency
ATV   see 4WD
DEC   New York State Department of Environmental Conservation
N–P   Northville–Placid (Trail)
PBM   Permanent Bench Mark

LEAVE NO TRACE

ADK supports the seven principles of the Leave No Trace program:

1. PLAN AHEAD AND PREPARE
   Know the regulations and special considerations for the area you'll visit. Prepare for extreme weather, hazards, and emergencies. Travel in groups of less than ten people to minimize impacts.
2. TRAVEL AND CAMP ON DURABLE SURFACES
   Hike in the middle of the trail; stay off of vegetation. Camp in designated sites where possible. In other areas, don't camp within 150 feet of water or a trail.
3. DISPOSE OF WASTE PROPERLY
   Pack out all trash (including toilet paper), leftover food, and litter. Use existing privies, or dig a cat hole five to six inches deep, then cover hole. Wash yourself and dishes at least 150 feet from water.
4. LEAVE WHAT YOU FIND
   Leave rocks, plants, and other natural objects as you find them. Let photos, drawings, or journals help to capture your memories. Do not build structures or furniture or dig trenches.
5. MINIMIZE CAMPFIRE IMPACTS
   Use a portable stove to avoid the lasting impact of a campfire. Where fires are permitted, use existing fire rings and only collect downed wood. Burn all fires to ash, put out campfires completely, then hide traces of fire.
6. RESPECT WILDLIFE
   Observe wildlife from a distance. Avoid wildlife during mating, nesting, and other sensitive times. Control pets at all times, and clean up after them.
7. BE CONSIDERATE OF OTHER VISITORS
   Respect other visitors and protect the quality of their experience. Let natural sounds prevail; avoid loud sounds and voices. Be courteous and yield to other users on the trail.

For further information on Leave No Trace principles, log on to www.lnt.org.

USGS	United States Geological Survey
4WD	Four-wheel-drive vehicle
ft	foot or feet
jct.	junction
km	kilometer or kilometers
m	meter or meters
mi	mile or miles
Rd.	Road
RR	railroad
yd	yard or yards

Maps

The trails in this guide are all illustrated on National Geographic *Trails Illustrated Map: Adirondack Park, #743, Lake George/Great Sacandaga* and *Trails Illustrated Map: Adirondack Park, #742, Lake Placid/High Peaks.*

The Trails Illustrated maps are letter-number coded, with letters running vertically on the sides of the map, and numbers running across the top and bottom of the maps (example: L29). Each trail's coordinate appears with the corresponding description in the book.

Each trail is numbered in this book and there is a corresponding trail number on the Trails Illustrated map. The maps also include a list of all trails shown on the map, including trails from other volumes in ADK's Forest Preserve Series. These numbers are not used on any signs on the trails.

Heavy black dashed lines indicate trails on the maps. In addition to showing trails, the maps include symbols for important items including lean-tos, campgrounds, boat launches, lookout towers, picnic areas, and more. See the map legend for complete details.

Trail mileages are indicated by small red teardrops and mileage numbers, rounded to the nearest tenth.

Extra copies of these maps are available from ADK (www.adk.org).

Trail Signs and Markers

Marked and maintained DEC trails for Adirondack hikers, cross-country skiers, snowshoers, and snowmobilers tend to have signs posted at

View from the summit of Black Mountain. CARL HEILMAN II

trailheads and major trail junctions. Trail signs give the distance to named locations on the trail. (See also Distance and Time, below, for discrepancies regarding distances.)

Trail markers are metal or plastic disks found on the trails themselves and on trail signs. The color and type of marker used on a trail is included in the descriptions in this book. (Painted blazes on trees generally indicate property boundaries and should not be confused with marked trails.)

With normal alertness to one's surroundings and exceptions made for lightly traveled trails, most Adirondack trails are easy to follow. Although this guidebook does mention particularly tricky turns or trails that might pose special difficulties, each hiker must remain alert at all times for changes of direction. Group leaders have a particular responsibility not to let inexperienced members of their party travel by themselves. A trail that seems obvious to a more experienced person may not be that way at all to an inexperienced member of the group.

It should go without saying that one should never remove any sign or marker. Hikers noticing damaged or missing signs should report this to:

Division of Lands and Forests
Dept. of Environmental Conservation
Ray Brook, NY 12977
518-897-1200

All trails described in this guide are on public land or public rights of way that cross private land. The continued goodwill of public-spirited Adirondack landowners is directly dependent upon the manner in which the public uses this land. The "posted" signs occasionally found on rights of way are usually intended to remind hikers that they are on private land over which the owner has granted permission for hikers to pass. In most cases, leaving the trail, camping, fishing, and hunting are not permitted on these lands. Hikers should respect the owner's wishes.

Distance and Time

Trails in this guidebook have been measured with a professional surveyor's wheel. Distances are expressed to the nearest tenth of a mile. Shorter distances are expressed as yards, and the number of yards has usually been derived from a wheel measurement in the field. In cases where there is disagreement between a sign and the guide's stated distance, the latter can be assumed correct. DEC has been informed of these discrepancies

At the start of each section of this guide, there is a list of trails in the region, the mileage unique to the trail, and the page on which the trail description begins. All mileages given in the trail description are cumulative, the beginning of the trail being the 0.0-mile point. A distance summary is given at the end of each description, with a total distance expressed in kilometers as well as in miles. If a trail has climbed significantly over its course, its total ascent in both feet and meters is provided.

To the inexperienced hiker, distances are likely to seem longer on the trail, depending on the weight of the pack, the time of day, and the frequency and degree of ascents and descents. He or she will quickly learn that there is a significant difference between "sidewalk miles" and "trail miles."

No attempt has been made to estimate travel time for these trails. A conservative rule to follow in estimating time is to allow an hour for every one and one-half miles, plus one half hour for each one thousand feet of ascent, letting experience indicate how close the individual hiker is to this standard. Most day hikers will probably go a little faster than this, but backpackers will probably find they go somewhat slower. Some quickening of pace usually occurs when descending, though this may not be true on steep descents.

Day Hiking and Wilderness Camping

It is not the purpose of this series to teach one how to hike or camp. The information below should, however, serve to make hikers aware of the differences and peculiarities of the Adirondacks while giving strong emphasis to currently recommended procedures for reducing environmental damage—particularly in heavily used areas. Users who intend to hike or camp for the first time are urged to consult a current book on the subject, attend one of the many workshops or training sessions available, or at least join a group led by someone with experience.

Except for Johns Brook Lodge, 3.5 miles up the Marcy Trail from Keene Valley (see *Adirondack Trails: High Peaks Region*), there are no huts in the Adirondacks for public use, such as are common in the White Mountains of New Hampshire. There are many lean-tos at convenient locations along trails and also many possibilities for tenting. The regulations regarding tenting and the use of lean-tos are simple

So What if it's Not Maintained?

A formal, DEC-marked trail and a bushwhack form the bookends of hiking possibilities in the Adirondacks—with lots more range in between than most hikers expect. Unmaintained trails, unmarked trails, "trailless" routes, or herd paths have two things in common: they are unmarked paths, lacking official DEC signs and markers, and they may necessitate advanced orientation skills.

Unmarked paths can range from reasonably well-trodden, well-defined routes with cairns to a whisper of a track with no discernable tread. A hiker's experience with one kind of unmarked path doesn't necessarily assist him or her on another. Hikers should carry a map and compass and know how to use them. They shouldn't let past experience inspire false confidence or tempt them to forego packing a map and compass.

and unrestrictive compared to those of other popular backpacking areas in this country and Canada. It is important that every backpacker know and obey the restrictions that do exist because they are designed to promote the long-term enjoyment and protection of the resource.

Listed below are some of the most important Forest preserve regulations, many of which pertain to day-hikers as well. These can also be found at www.dec.ny.gov/outdoor/7872.html. Complete regulations are available from the DEC and are posted at most trail access points.

• Except where marked by a "Camp Here" disk, camping is prohibited within 150 feet of roads, trails, lakes, ponds, streams, or other bodies of water.

• Groups of ten or more persons (nine in the High Peaks Region) or stays of more than three days in one place require a permit from the New York State Forest Ranger responsible for the area.

• Lean-tos are available in many areas on a first-come, first-served basis. Lean-tos cannot be used exclusively and must be shared with other campers. (See also page 22.)

• Use pit privies provided near popular camping areas and trailheads. If none are available, dispose of human waste by digging a hole six to eight inches deep at least 150 feet from water or campsites. Cover with leaves and soil.

- Do not use soap to wash yourself, clothing, or dishes within 150 feet of water.
- Fires should be built in existing fire pits or fireplaces if provided. Use only dead and down wood for fires. Cutting standing trees is prohibited. Extinguish all fires with water and stir ashes until they are cold to the touch. Do not build fires in areas marked by a "No Fires" disk. Camp stoves are safer, more efficient, and cleaner.
- Carry out what you carry in. Use Leave No Trace practices (see p. 16).
- Keep your pet under control. Restrain it on a leash when others approach. Collect and bury droppings away from water, trails, and campsites. Keep your pet away from drinking water sources.
- Observe and enjoy wildlife and plants but leave them undisturbed.
- Removing plants, rocks, fossils, or artifacts from state land without a permit is illegal.
- Do not feed any wild animals.
- Store food properly to keep it away from animals—particularly bears.
- No camping is permitted above 4000 feet (1219 meters) at any time of the year in the Adirondacks.
- Except in an emergency or between December 21 and March 21, camping is prohibited above an elevation of 3500 feet in the Catskills.
- At all times, only emergency fires are permitted above 4000 feet in the Adirondacks and 3500 feet in the Catskills.

CELL PHONES

Cell phones should not be relied upon in case of emergency. Despite several highly publicized stories, their use in the backcountry is limited by terrain, distance from communication towers, and other factors. Those who carry them should, out of consideration for their fellow hikers, use them only when necessary—and should have alternative plans for handling emergencies in case they do not operate.

Lean-tos

Lean-tos are available on a first-come, first-served basis up to the capacity of the shelter—usually about eight persons. Thus a small party cannot claim exclusive use of a shelter and must allow late arrivals equal use. Most lean-tos have a fireplace in front (sometimes with a primitive grill) and sanitary facilities. Most are located near some source of water, but each camper must use his or her own judgment as to whether or not the water supply needs purification before drinking. It is in very poor taste to carve or write one's initials in a shelter. Please try to keep these rustic shelters in good condition and appearance.

Because reservations cannot be made for any of these shelters, it is best to carry a tent or other alternate shelter. Many shelters away from the standard routes, however, are seldom used, and a small party can often find a shelter open in the more remote areas.

The following regulations apply specifically to lean-tos, in addition to the general camping regulations listed above:
• No plastic may be used to close off the front of a shelter.
• No nails or other permanent fastener may be used to affix a tarp in a lean-to, but it is permissible to use rope to tie canvas or nylon tarps across the front.
• No tent may be pitched inside a lean-to.

Groups
Any group of ten or more persons or smaller groups intending to camp at one location three nights or longer must obtain a permit before camping on state land. This system is designed to prevent overuse of certain critical sites and also to encourage groups to split into smaller parties.

Permits can be obtained from the DEC forest ranger closest to the actual starting point of one's proposed trip. The local forest ranger can be contacted by writing directly; if in doubt about whom to write, send the letter to the DEC Lands and Forests Division Office address for the county in which your trip will take place (refer to DEC addresses in

Trail Signs and Markers section). They will forward the letter to the proper ranger, but write early enough to permit a response before your trip date.

One can also make the initial contact with the forest ranger by telephone. Note that forest rangers' schedules during the busy summer season are often unpredictable. Forest rangers are listed in the white pages of local phone books under "New York, State of; Environmental Conservation, Department of; Forest Ranger." Bear in mind when calling that most rangers operate out of their private homes; observe the normal courtesy used when calling a private residence. Contact by letter is much preferred. Camping with a large group requires careful planning with a lead time of several weeks to ensure a happy, safe outing.

Forest Safety

The routes described in this guidebook vary from wide, well-marked DEC trails to narrow, unmarked footpaths that have become established through long use. With normal alertness and careful preparation the hiker should have few problems in land navigation. Nevertheless, careful map study and route planning are fundamental necessities. Hikers should never expect immediate help should an emergency occur. This is particularly true in winter, when fewer people are on the trails and weather is a more significant factor.

In addition to a map, all hikers should carry a compass and know at least the basics of its use. In some descriptions, the Forest Preserve Series uses compass bearings to differentiate trails at a junction or to indicate the direction of travel above timberline. More important, a compass can be an indispensable aid in the event that you lose your way.

Winter trips, especially, must be carefully planned. Travel over ice on ski and snowshoe trips must be done with caution. The possibility of freezing rain, snow, and cold temperatures should be considered from early September until late May. True winter conditions can commence as early as November and last well into April, particularly at higher altitudes. It is highly recommended that hikers travel in parties of at least four people, be outfitted properly, rest when the need arises, and drink plenty of water. Leave trip plans with someone at home and then keep to your itinerary.

Drinking Water

For many years, hikers could trust almost any water source in the Adirondacks to be pure and safe to drink. Unfortunately, as in many other mountain areas, some Adirondack water sources have become contaminated with a parasite known as *Giardia lamblia*.

This intestinal parasite causes a disease known as giardiasis—often called "beaver fever." It can be spread by any warm-blooded mammal when infected feces wash into the water; beavers are prime agents in transferring this parasite because they spend so much of their time in and near water. Hikers themselves have also become primary agents in spreading this disease because some individuals appear to be unaffected carriers of the disease, and other recently infected individuals may inadvertently spread the parasite before their symptoms become apparent.

Prevention: Follow the guidelines for the disposal of human excrement as stated in Other Regulations, above. Equally important, make sure that every member of your group is aware of the problem and follows the guidelines as well. The health of a fellow hiker may depend on your consideration.

Water Treatment: No water source can be guaranteed to be safe. Boil all water for 2–3 minutes, utilize an iodine-based chemical purifier (available at camping supply stores and some drug and department stores), or use a commercial filter designed specifically for giardiasis prevention. If after returning from a trip you experience recurrent

BIG-GAME SEASONS IN THE ADIRONDACKS ARE USUALLY AS FOLLOWS:

- **Early Bear Season:** Begins the first Saturday after the second Monday in September and continues for four weeks.
- **Archery Season** (deer and bear): September 27 to opening of the regular season.
- **Muzzle-loading Season** (deer and bear): The seven days prior to the opening of regular season.
- **Regular Season:** Next-to-last Saturday in October through the first Sunday in December.

On occasion, special situations require DEC to modify the usual dates of hunting seasons.

ADK does not promote hunting as one of its organized activities, but it does recognize that sport hunting, when carried out in compliance with the game laws administered by the DEC, is a legitimate sporting activity.

intestinal problems, consult your physician and explain your potential problem.

Hunting Seasons

Unlike the national park system, public lands within the Adirondack and Catskill state parks are open to sport hunting. There are separate rules and seasons for each type of hunting (small game, waterfowl, and big game), but it is the big-game season, i.e., deer and bear, that is most likely to concern hikers. Confrontations can occur when hikers and hunters are inconsiderate of the needs and rights of each other. Problems can be greatly reduced by careful planning.

It is advisable to avoid heavily hunted areas during big-game seasons. Because it is difficult to carry a deer or bear carcass long distances or over steep terrain, hikers will find few hunters more than a mile from a roadway or in rugged mountain country. Lower slopes of beech, maple, and hemlock have much more hunting pressure than cripplebush, spruce, and balsam fir on upper slopes. Motorized vehicles are not allowed in areas designated as Wilderness, so hike there; most areas designated as Wild Forest have woods roads where vehicles can be used, so avoid these areas, which are likely to be favored by hunters. Try to avoid the opening and closing day of regular deer season. For safety, wear a bright-colored outer garment; orange is recommended.

Bear Safety

Most wildlife in the Adirondacks and Catskills are little more than a minor nuisance around the campsite. Generally, the larger the animal the more timid it is in the presence of humans. Some animals are emboldened by the aroma of food, however, and bears, the most intimidating of these, quickly habituate to human food sources.

The following tips will reduce the likelihood of an encounter with a bear.

• Never keep food in your tent or lean-to.

• DEC now requires campers to use bear-resistant canisters in the Eastern Zone of the High Peaks Wilderness between April 1 and November 30.

• In other areas, use a canister or hang food at least fifteen feet off the ground from a rope strung between two trees that are at least fifteen feet apart and one hundred feet from the campsite. (Hangs using a branch have a high failure rate.) Using dark-colored rope tied off five or more feet above the ground makes it less likely that a foraging bear will see the line or find it while sniffing along the ground.

• Wrap aromatic foods well.

• Plan carefully to keep trash and leftovers to a minimum. Wrap in sealed containers such as large Ziploc bags, and hang or place in canister.

• Hang your pack, along with clothing worn during cooking.

• Keep a garbage-free fire pit away from your camping area.

• Should a bear appear, do not provoke it by throwing objects or approaching it.

ADK ARCHIVES

BEAR CANISTERS

Bears in many parts of the Adirondacks have figured out the long-popular campers' technique of hanging food from a rope strung between two trees. Thus the DEC is now recommending—in some cases strongly encouraging—the use of bear-resistant, food-storage canisters. Bear-resistant canisters are required to be used by overnight campers in the Eastern High Peaks Wilderness between April 1 and November 30.

Bear-resistant canisters can be obtained from many outdoor retailers, borrowed from many ADK chapters, or rented or purchased at ADK's Heart Lake or Lake George facilities. The canisters also protect food from many smaller forest creatures.

The DEC's current management goal with respect to bears is to educate campers about proper food storage. Bears unable to get food from campers will, it is hoped, return to their natural diet. Thus campers play an important role in helping to restore the natural balance between bears and humans. Losing one's food to a bear should be recognized as a critical failure in achieving this goal.

Bang pots, blow a whistle, shout, or otherwise try to drive it off with sharp noises. Should this fail, leave the scene.
• Report bear encounters to a forest ranger.

Rabies Alert

Rabies infestation has been moving north through New York State. Although it is most often associated with raccoons, any warm-blooded mammal can be a carrier.

Although direct contact with a rabid animal in the forest is not likely, some precautions are advisable:
• Do not feed or pet any wild animals, under any circumstances.
• Particularly avoid any wild animals that seem to be behaving strangely.
• If bitten by a wild animal, seek medical attention immediately.

Insect-Borne Diseases

Although not unique to the Adirondacks and Catskills, two insects found in these areas carry potentially lethal diseases. Deer ticks can

EMERGENCY PROCEDURES

For all emergencies in Region 5, call the DEC 24-hour hotline: 518-891-0235.

All emergency assistance, including help from the local ranger, is dispatched from this number. Make sure the person going for help has the telephone number as well as a complete written description of the type and exact location of the accident. A location marked on the map can be very helpful. If possible, leave a call-back number in the event those responding to the incident require additional information.

Calling the above number is preferable to calling 911. At the DEC emergency number, the caller is usually able to speak directly with someone who is knowledgeable about the area where the accident has occurred. Cell phone callers are especially prone to problems because the call may be picked up by a distant tower in a neighboring jurisdiction (or even a different state) with the message then having to be relayed through several agencies.

Other DEC Region 5, Ray Brook contacts:
General information: 518-897-1200
Rangers: 518-897-1300
Environmental conservation officers: 518-897-1326

---

spread Lyme disease, and mosquitos can transmit West Nile virus. These are issues of particular concern in the Catskills.

In both instances, protection is advisable. Wear long pants and long-sleeved shirts and apply an insect repellent with the recommended percentage of N, N-diethyl-meta-toluamide (commonly known as DEET). On returning home, thoroughly inspect yourself and wash yourself and your clothing immediately. Seek immediate attention if any early symptoms (rash, long-term fatigue, headache, fever) arise. ◆

Valcour Island on Lake Champlain. CARL HEILMAN II

Northern Section

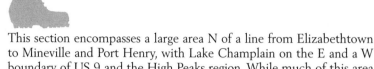

This section encompasses a large area N of a line from Elizabethtown to Mineville and Port Henry, with Lake Champlain on the E and a W boundary of US 9 and the High Peaks region. While much of this area is owned by private landowners and timber companies, there are a number of fine trails with great diversity in terrain. From Valcour Island in the extreme NE corner of the Adirondack Park, to the Split Rock Mt. area which contains the longest undeveloped shoreline on Lake Champlain, this area offers some unusual Adirondack experiences.

While trails are well suited for the beginning hiker, the veteran hiker may find exploring some of the trailless rocky crags and outlooks an unexpected challenge. There are also two wildlife management areas just north of Port Kent: Ausable Marsh State Wildlife Management Area, and Wickham Marsh Wildlife Management Area. There is both hiking and canoeing in these two regions.

❊ Trails in winter: In a good snow year, most trails in the region's northern section are suitable for snowshoeing and skiing. However, since most of these trails are at lower elevations and many are near Lake Champlain, snow conditions will deteriorate more quickly than in the rest of the Adirondacks. It is advisable to carry instep crampons in case of icy conditions. These suggestions are for all trails in the region unless otherwise noted.

SHORT HIKE:
• Belfry Mt.—0.4 mi (0.6 km). A short, easy walk to an open summit and climbable fire tower with views of Mineville, the Adirondacks, and the Green Mts. in Vermont.

MODERATE HIKE:
• Valcour Island Perimeter Trail—5.7 mi (9.1 km). Spectacular views on all sides as you circle the island. There are several ways to shorten this loop via interior trails.

HARDER HIKE:
• Split Rock Mt. Circuit—8.8 mi (14.2 km). Split Rock Mt. North

Rim Trail, returning via Robin's Run Trail to Louis Clearing Bay Trail and a side trip down and back up the Bay Trail. Woods, a mountaintop, and shoreline views of Lake Champlain.

VALCOUR ISLAND

Trails Illustrated #742: JJ31-32

Valcour Island is a jewel in Lake Champlain. The island itself is varied and fascinating, with coves that offer good anchorage for boaters and pleasant, easy trails that often give the hiker spectacular views of the Adirondacks and Vermont's Green Mountains. Rocky shelves provide excellent seats to watch crashing waves on the E side, as well as a lovely, quiet sandy beach on the W side. The island, which gave its name to an important battle in the Revolutionary War (see below), is about 980 acres.

All trails are marked with special Valcour Island yellow disks. The Perimeter Trail (trail 1) circles the island in 5.7 mi; two interior trails (trails 2 and 3) combine for a total of 7.8 mi of trails on the island. Campsites are well kept and in idyllic settings. The thorn among these roses is the profusion of poison ivy on the island.

▶Trailhead: From the former Air Force Base entrance on US 9, just S of downtown Plattsburgh, drive S 4.5 mi to the Peru Boat Launch. Coming from the S, from the jct. of US 9 and NY 22 in Keeseville, drive N on US 9 8.8 mi to the Peru Boat Launch. From Exit 35 (Peru–Valcour) on the Northway (I-87), take Rte. 422 (Bear Swamp Rd.) E 3 mi to US 9, and turn L (N) 3.3 mi to the Peru Boat Launch. ◀

THERE IS A PARKING LOT and public bathroom at the Peru Boat Launch site. On a summer Saturday a parade of cars and trucks back trailers down the ramp to unload motorboats. Many of these people seem to be families headed to Butterfly Beach for picnics and swimming on Valcour (which means "almost one rock" in French).

A warning: Lake Champlain's deep waters are notorious for being cold. Huge waves can sweep across the lake on rough days. Do not use a canoe in cold weather or if the water is rough. Hypothermia can set in quickly. Late summer is the best time for a canoe crossing. In winter when the lake is frozen it is possible to ski across, observing proper safety precautions.

It is almost exactly 1.0 mi E from the boat launch to Bullhead Bay, a pleasant, grassy place just S of the old lighthouse where hikers can pull up their boats and find the Perimeter Trail almost immediately. Or they can go NE around the point to Butterfly Bay and pull up on the sandy beach.

The DEC officer who patrols the island from a boat gives out maps of the island that show the hiking trails, names of bays, campsites, and rules. Those planning to camp on the island must register with him upon landing, or on his rounds.

(1) **Perimeter Trail**

Trails Illustrated Map #742: JJ31-32

The following describes a hike around the island on the yellow-marked Perimeter Trail (trail 1) starting S from Bullhead Bay, although the trail can just as easily be hiked in the other direction. Two interior trails (trails 2 and 3, below) create numerous options.

FROM BULLHEAD BAY (0.0 mi) walk inland from the beach about 50 ft through the woods to the Perimeter Trail. Turn R, heading S. The trail crosses an open meadow, then a small foot bridge. Then, from poplars and poison ivy, the trail enters cedar woods, reaching a jct. at 0.3 mi with signs indicating Indian Point (R) and the Nomad Trail (trail 2) to Smugglers Harbor (L).

A short trail to the R leads to a large, open clearing with two fireplaces, a privy, and a good campsite above lovely Indian Point. The stone shelves are excellent for picnicking, swimming, and play. Campsites 2, 3, and 4 are also here, offering good views of the Adirondacks. In August, invasive purple loosestrife grows between the cracks in the shelving rock. Numerous light yellow butterflies attend to business among these flowers.

Continuing S, the Perimeter Trail enters cool, deep woods of white cedar, white and red pine, maple, oak, ash, spruce, wild grapes, and giant poison ivy. At 0.5 mi a large dead spruce tree bears a sign, "American Revolution, Battle of Valcour, October 11, 1776." On that date a small American fleet led by Gen. Benedict Arnold hid behind the W side of the island and surprised a larger British fleet heading S down the lake, led by Captain Thomas Pringle. The British fleet chased the Americans for two days S to Ticonderoga and destroyed Arnold's brash brigade of boats. Despite this loss, Arnold won a tactical victory by delaying the British, forcing them to return to Canada for the winter. This extra time gave the American troops at Saratoga a chance to build up men and supplies, which resulted in their victory there on October 17, 1777. History buffs revel in the imagined sight of Arnold's tiny, gutsy fleet rounding the S tip of Valcour to ruin what Pringle thought would be an unchallenged trip up Lake Champlain.

It is about 50 ft R to a grassy overlook on a cliff with an excellent view of Whiteface Mt. and of interesting fissures in the shoreline limestone rock into a stand of cedars and out into a meadow. The trail crosses a footbridge at a little over 0.6 mi and at 0.7 mi reaches campsite 1 (with privy) on Cedar Point. This is a smooth rocky promontory.

The trail onward is over a broad, solid rock incline going into cedar, hemlock, and birch woods. A long elbow-shaped cement dock comes into view on the R through trees. At 0.8 mi, the beautiful old stone "Seton House" with its slate roof offers a path from its front R corner to a pumphouse, dock, and point. One may walk on the dock, or picnic, but mooring a boat here is prohibited.

At 1.0 mi on the Perimeter Trail, a turn R on a faint track leads to high cliffs with spectacular views S and E of Lake Champlain, the Green Mts., and the Adirondacks. There is loose gravel here, so stay away from the edge and find a firm footing. This is not a recommended spot for acrophobics.

The Perimeter Trail continues around the S side of the island through deep, cool cedar woods with chickadees. At 1.4 mi it curves L (N) along the E side of the island. At about 1.5 mi, there is a sign to Pebble Beach on the R, a steep trail descending to a cozy beach surrounded by fantastic metamorphic cliffs on either side. Beach stones are rounded and smooth from wave action. This is the closest view of nearby Garden Island.

The Perimeter Trail continues through oak, ash, and maple woods. At 1.7 mi there is a turn R off the trail to a SE promontory, and at 1.8 mi there is a 20-ft cliff facing E to Vermont.

The trail now curves W along the shore around a wide cove with shelving rock. There is a good view here of Grand Isle in Vermont. At 1.9 mi the trail reaches small but spectacular Cystid Point, with campsite 18 (cement fireplace, table, and privy). At 2.0 mi there is a wooden walkway, then a rocky shelf beach, excellent for swimming.

At 2.4 mi, a small foot trail leads R to a rocky overlook above a small cove that offers a good mooring. Just N, at 2.6 mi, there is another campsite; across a wooden walkway is a fenced area around a large beach rock in memory of the captain of the ship Nomad, Gerald Walker Birks, "who sailed these waters many years and found safe harbour in this cove" and of "four members of the crew who fought with Canadian and Imperial Forces 1914–1918."

At 2.7 mi, at a trail jct., a turn R leads to Smugglers Harbor in a few hundred yards, or L to return to Indian Point on the W side of the island via the Nomad Trail (trail 2), 0.8 mi. Campsites 15, 16, and 17 are along Smugglers Harbor. Hikers may continue along the Perimeter Trail to the next jct. for Tiger Point (0.1 mi), or take a more interesting route 0.2 mi from campsite 15 N along the shore to Tiger Point and back inland to the Perimeter Trail. The strange shape of Tiger Point makes interesting exploring.

From the Tiger Point jct., the Perimeter Trail swings around Sloop Bay, where there is a privy.

At 3.2 mi, at another trail jct., it is 0.1 mi straight ahead on a spur to Paradise Bay. Down this spur are an old fireplace and chimney and campsite 13. A larger, more beautiful stone fireplace and chimney on the point suggest that this must have been a site for a house. Campsite 14 overlooks the lake to Spoon Island.

Soon after the Paradise Bay turn-off, the Perimeter Trail descends through cool cedar woods to a jct. at 3.4 mi. A spur R leads to Spoon Bay in a few hundred ft. The Perimeter Trail reaches another jct. in about 250 ft; here the Royal Savage Trail (trail 3) turns L (W) to cross the interior of the island to Butterfly Bay.

The Perimeter Trail veers R to continue N, going uphill through hemlocks, then leveling out at 3.7 mi overlooking Spoon Bay. At 3.8 mi there is another overlook, this time over Beauty Bay. The trail turns L and then R downhill over a wooden bridge through giant evergreens to another wooden bridge, then reaches campsites 10 and 11.

Now the trail goes through giant white pines, and at 4.1 mi reaches a sandy beach on the N edge of the island. Crab Island is straight N. On a mainland bluff to the W is Clinton Community College; the large white building was at one time President William McKinley's Summer White House. Just before 4.4 mi there are five more campsites: 5, 6, 7, 8, and 9. This is Island's End.

The trail now heads S. At 4.8 mi there are several giant white oaks, then a large overgrown pasture, then at 4.9 mi a privy. Now the trail turns L under a huge canopy hedge to a "Pioneer Farm Site" sign in a pasture at 5.0 mi. This is now a huge open pasture with raspberries and goldfinches in summer. From the edge of the pasture one can see the Peru Boat Launch with Whiteface Mt. directly behind.

At 5.2 mi, the trail crosses a wooden bridge surrounded by poison ivy. At 5.3 mi, there is another well-built wooden bridge, then at 5.4

mi a sign, "Island's End," pointing N.

Now the trail enters a lovely mown clearing with shade trees and 10 fireplaces and picnic tables on the N edge of the beach on Butterfly Bay. Turn L (E) to find the trail again. The Royal Savage Trail (trail 3) to Spoon Bay (1.3 mi) starts behind the privy on the back of the clearing. The Perimeter Trail returns to its starting point at Bullhead Bay at 5.7 mi, where a trail R (W) leads to a point with an historic 1874 stone lighthouse. (There is also a trail S from Butterfly Beach and W to the lighthouse. At 0.2 mi along this trail, one fork goes L to Bullhead Bay in 0.1 mi and the goes R to the lighthouse in 0.2 mi).

🜨 Distances: Peru Boat Launch to Bullhead Bay via boat, 1.0 mi; Bullhead Bay to stone house, 0.8 mi; to Pebble Beach trail, 1.5 mi; to Nomad Trail (trail 2) jct., 2.7 mi; to Royal Savage Trail (trail 3) jct., 3.4 mi; to Island's End, 4.4 mi; to pioneer farm site, 5.0 mi; to Bullhead Bay, 5.7 mi (9.1 km).

(2) Nomad Trail

Trails Illustrated Map #742: JJ31-32

THE TWO INTERIOR TRAILS add up to another 2.1 mi of hiking on Valcour Island. The shorter trail, on the S, is the Nomad Trail (0.8 mi), which connects Indian Point on the W and Smugglers Harbor on the E. This is a beautiful deep-woods trail with gigantic white and red pine, cedar, hemlock, maple, birch, and oak.

From the Indian Point jct. on the Perimeter Trail (trail 1) (0.0 mi), the trail goes E 0.6 mi to a wooden walkway, at 0.7 mi crosses another wooden walkway, and at 0.8 mi meets the Perimeter Trail on the E side of the island. Straight ahead is Smugglers Harbor, R (S) is Cystid Point, and L (N) is Sloop Bay.

🜨 Distance: Indian Point to Smugglers Harbor, 0.8 mi (1.3 km).

(3) Royal Savage Trail

Trails Illustrated Map #742: JJ31-32

THE TRAIL TO THE L at 3.4 mi on the Perimeter Trail (trail 1) is the Royal Savage Trail, which goes 1.3 mi W through the northern interior of the island to Butterfly Bay. Leaving the Perimeter Trail (0.0 mi), at first it passes through deep woods, then through an open field, then across a wooden walkway into mature white pine, cedar, birch, and hemlock. After a second wooden bridge, the trail emerges into an open area with wild fruit trees, then sumac, then into deep woods again, then into another overgrown field. After passing through a tree-shaded picnic area, it reaches the W Perimeter Trail at Butterfly Bay. A loop using both interior trails equals 3.5 mi.

🐾 Distance: Royal Savage Trail, 1.3 mi (2.1 km).

(4) Poke-O-Moonshine Mt.

Trails Illustrated Map #742: EE30

This fire tower peak is extremely popular because of its views of Lake Champlain and of the High Peaks in the distance to the SW. Its unusual name appears to be a combination of two Algonquin words, "Pohqui" and "Moosie," which mean, respectively, "broken" and "smooth." The name, later corrupted by the early settlers, seems to refer to the smooth rocks of the summit or the prominent slab on the SE side and the broken rocks of the impressive cliff on the E side. The woods were extensively damaged by a January 1998 ice storm. The heavily-used trail is wide and eroded in places and undergoing a long-term repair and hardening effort by ADK and DEC. They and a local group, the Friends of Poke-O-Moonshine, have developed 11 interpretive stops keyed to a brochure available at the trail register. The fire tower has been renovated and is open and staffed by a Summit Steward five days a week during the summer.

▶ Trailhead: The trail starts at the state campground on Rte. 9, 9.3 mi N of the jct. of the road from Lewis to Exit 32 on the Adirondack Northway (I-87) and 3.0 mi S of Exit 33. There is a parking fee charged at this facility, and parking on the highway in front of the campground is prohibited. This presents no problem in the off-season, but hikers should either be prepared to pay this fee or to walk a few hundred yards extra from outside the "no parking" zone. ◀

STARTING FROM THE S END of the campground (0.0 mi), the red-marked trail enters the woods and immediately begins climbing, steeply at times, to the base of a cliff at 0.3 mi. Skirting the cliff on the L, the trail switchbacks R to a good lookout on the R at just over 0.3 mi. The grade now eases somewhat but remains steady to a saddle S of the summit at 0.8 mi. Here are the remains of the fire observer's cabin with a lean-to approx. 65 yd to the L.

Poke-O-Moonshine Mt. firetower. NANCIE BATTAGLIA

From this saddle the trail heads R up a steep, washed-out bank. It leads up past a lookout on the L and along a shelf before turning R and up to the summit plateau. Turning R again, the trail goes through open woods to the summit and tower at 1.2 mi.

❋ Trail in winter: Not suitable for skiing; very steep for snowshoers.

⚲ Distances: Campground to summit of Poke-O-Moonshine, 1.2 mi (1.9 km). Ascent, 1280 ft (390 m). Elevation, 2180 ft (664 m).

SPLIT ROCK MT. AREA

Trails Illustrated Map #742: AA32-33

The Split Rock Mt. area N of Westport on Lake Champlain, encompassing trails 6–11B of this guidebook, is a beautiful but little-used region purchased over many years by the state. The most recent acquisition was made in 1993 as the inaugural purchase under New York State's Environmental Protection Fund, saving the tract from a second-home development.

As of January 2008, there are seven marked trails in the area, on a system of old tote roads leading out from a parking lot on state land. Several loops are possible. Some flagging has also been placed on the main trails. A management plan is being developed for the region, so it is likely that a state trail system will be marked in the near future. The trail that traverses the rock ledges over the top of Split Rock Mt. is one of the more spectacular in the region. There are new signs at most of the trail jcts., but not all, so close attention to this guidebook and its map is advised.

For those interested in viewing wildlife, just NW across the Lake Shore Rd., and slightly N, is Webb Royce Swamp. There are no trails here, but the area is not far from the road and is inhabited by a variety of wildlife. Check the trailhead map for directions.

While parts of this region were at one time developed and logged, there are few remnants of that period in the S half of this tract, except for the old logging roads and stonework from an old granite mine. The N half (from the current trail access N to the private land boundary) has seen more recent timber activities. It is this complexity of logging roads that forms the backbone of the future trail system. This segment was also worked for both granite and iron ore over a century ago, and there are remnants of these activities in a couple of places.

The forest is characterized by the lower-elevation flora of an open hardwood forest, with oaks and juniper trees on the rocky bluffs and hemlocks growing densely along the cool, moist streambeds. This area is within the historic range of the timber rattlesnake, so it is wise to use caution when traveling over open rocky areas and the densely grassy areas on some of the roads as there are snakes still calling this area home. Never tease or corner a rattler. If you give them a wide berth and leave them alone, they will leave you alone. Eastern timber rattlesnakes are protected under New York State law. It is illegal to kill, take, or possess this species without a special DEC permit.

▶ Trailhead: Four of the seven trails in the Split Rock Mt. network utilize a single trailhead, which also serves as overflow parking for the fifth trail (trail 6). From Exit 31 on the Northway (I-87), head E on NY 9N to the intersection of NY 22 in Westport in 4.2 mi. Turn L (N) onto NY 22 (0.0 mi) and in 0.4 mi turn R (NE) onto Lake Shore Rd. At 0.9 mi bear R (E) at the Y with Sherman Rd. Continue on (N) past Halds Rd. and Ainger Hill Rd. on the L (W), reaching the parking lot on the R with a Forest Preserve sign at 4.7 mi from the NY 9N/NY 22 intersection. ◀

(6) Calamity Trail

Trails Illustrated Map #742: AA32

▶ Trailhead: This trail starts E from the Lake Shore Rd., at 4.0 mi N from the jct. of NY 9N and NY 22 in Westport, in an overgrown field across from a gray farmhouse. There may be space to park a car or two on the shoulder, but be careful of the ditch. Otherwise, park 0.8 mi N at the main trailhead parking lot for the Split Rock Mt. area (see above). A parking lot is planned for this location in the future. ◀

In 2005, the start of this trail was not marked; red markers do start at the jct. with the Crossover Trail (10A). As an old road, it is generally easy to follow, except in two spots where it skirts wetlands. It used to serve as access to the 19th-century granite works at its E end, near Barn Rock Bay; both of these are interesting, unique destinations. This access became possible with a small state purchase of the field in the fall of 1998.

Go over the fence E at the old gate (0.0 mi) on a brushy tractor trail. The route heads along the S edge of the field and enters pine woods at 0.2 mi, heading gradually uphill, passing some swatches of 1998 ice storm damage. It reaches a height of land at 0.7 mi in mixed woods and passes a gate on the R before heading downhill. The yellow-marked jct. with the Crossover Trail is at this point. Red markers, heading E on the Calamity Trail, begin here.

The road narrows and contours R (S) around a wetland, passing a log barricade blocking off the old route. There are views into the swamp on the L, and then the trail bears R at a beaver dam between two arms of the wetland at 1.1 mi.

The path widens again into a roadway through mixed forest, passing between two small vernal pools at 1.5 mi at the base of a hill. It skirts a second wetland at this point, sneaking around its S side between grasses and a wooded bank.

The trail quickly jogs N over a small hummock and then E again, before passing some broken granite on the L. It reenters the woods, crossing a swampy outlet, and resumes its road-like character with the outlet stream on the R. There are numerous granite retaining walls on the L, the first signs of the old quarry whose block piles now become obvious everywhere. Keep a careful eye out for snakes if you are tempted to explore these heaps of granite.

The trail steepens down to a T intersection at 2.5 mi. The fork R (S) heads to private property in 0.3 mi. The fork L passes more granite piles and heads N to a jct. with the Barn Rock Trail (trail 10), over a small granite bridge at 2.8 mi. The way R leads to Barn Rock Bay in 0.2 mi. The trail L leads back to the main network of trails, 7–9A, and the main trailhead parking lot.

✳ Trail in winter: The trail is mostly wide and smooth for good skiing on less than a foot of snow; there are a couple of fast hills at the E end, but with plenty of room to maneuver. Snowshoeing is fine.

ᴍ Distances: Lake Shore Rd. to woods, 0.2 mi; to height of land, 0.7 mi; to first wetland crossing, 1.1 mi; to vernal pools, 1.5 mi; to T intersection, 2.5 mi; to Barn Rock Trail, 2.8 mi (4.5 km).

(7) **Split Rock Mountain North Rim Trail**

Trails Illustrated Map #742: AA33

▶ Trailhead: This trail starts at 0.3 mi along the Louis Clearing Bay Trail (trail 9), and forks L from it at a "Motorized Vehicles Prohibited" sign and two trail signs with yellow DEC markers. ◀

THE TRAIL BEGINS (0.0 mi) gradually and smoothly as a roadway but soon becomes an undulating exploration of the balds, wet dips, ridges, open woods, and summits of Split Rock Mt. as it winds N to a final lookout at 2.8 mi. It is cut out as an old logging road along its entire length and is marked by yellow disks. It can be combined as a loop with the Robin's Run Blue Trail (trail 8).

A quick rise at the start flattens out through second-growth woods as the trail passes rusted machinery and an overgrown jct. on the R. It takes a sharp turn uphill to the R at 0.4 mi (0.7 mi from the parking lot) at a jct. with a wet shortcut to the start of the Robin's Run Blue Trail (trail 8), which heads L. The trail rises R with yellow markers and steepens over a small lookout spot with some views to the N and then descends quickly to a grassy wet area at the far base of the hill at 0.6 mi. (The Blue Trail is just a few yards L through the wet grass.)

A 90-degree R turn takes the yellow trail to the E. It winds gradually uphill with occasional wet spots and bowed-over birches as it heads generally N. The trail traverses side hills and passes many stumps and second growth, with winter views to the NW.

At 1.5 mi, a rocky promontory is visible to the R above the trail, as it climbs quite steeply to a jct. R at a small hand-lettered sign, "View", at 1.8 mi. It is a short walk R up and over two bumps to a spectacular lookout over Lake Champlain.

The main trail continues uphill and N to a second lookout on the L over farms, the Jay Range, and Poke-O-Moonshine at 1.9 mi, then continues on a mostly rolling course on the W side of the ridge. The high point of the mountain, approx. 940 ft above Lake Champlain, is in this vicinity, though the trail makes no claim of attaining its wooded location. There are glimpses R (E) of the lake, from ridgetop portions of the trail, of woodlands with extensive 1998 ice storm damage.

At 2.6 mi, the trail meets the Robin's Run Trail (trail 8) straight on, and forks R (E). It meanders through semi-open woods with more glimpses of the lake on the R. It crosses a small rise or two, bearing N now, dead-ending at several yellow markers and a "Danger" sign at 2.8 mi. The views to the N over Whallons Bay and down Lake Champlain are well worth it.

✳ Trail in winter: The trail is wide enough for skiing and is mostly gentle, though the steep, twisty, and narrow "screamer" hill just S of the two lookouts at 1.8 mi necessitates deep snow and strong skiing skills or a descent on foot.

﷼ Distances: Louis Clearing Bay Trail to Robin's Run Trail, 0.4 mi; to sharp R at base of hill, 0.6 mi; to rocky lookout on R, 1.5 mi; to "View" sign, 1.8 mi; to N jct. with Robin's Run Trail, 2.6 mi; to final lookout at yellow markers, 2.8 mi (4.5 km) (3.1 mi/5.0 km from trailhead).

(8) Robin's Run Trail

Trails Illustrated Map #742: AA33

▶ Trailhead: This trail starts from the Split Rock Mt. North Rim Trail (trail 7), forking L from it at 0.4 mi, or 0.7 mi from the trailhead. ◀

THE TRAIL IS A MORE WESTERLY lowland approach to the N end of the Split Rock Range, climbing significantly only in its last 0.5 mi to the ridge, where it rejoins the same yellow-marked Split Rock Mt. North Rim Trail. The two trails can best be combined as a loop, going in either direction. In the spring of 2005, this trail was only sporadically marked with blue disks, most of them on the N sides of trees; with a minimum of care at two jcts., however, it is easy to follow.

At 0.7 mi from the parking lot, by way of the Louis Clearing Bay Trail (trail 9) and then the Split Rock Mt. North Rim Trail (trail 7), the Robin's Run Trail starts L with blue trail markers at a fork (0.0 mi). It is flat along a wet grassy stretch for 0.1 mi and then bears R, heading down on a long sidehill to an old logging clearing on the flat at 0.5 mi. The trail bears R (N) at the clearing on a grassy path and crosses a small culvert. It becomes more of a woods road on a rising straightaway and passes a large rocky outcrop on the R.

The trail bears slightly L and becomes more rolling at 0.7 mi, on a sidehill course. At 0.8 mi it passes an old logging road on the R and bent-over birches. It reaches a fork at 1.0 mi at an old bare sign, R, on a medium-sized pine.

The trail becomes narrower with many cut logs and the rocky hillside immediately R. Views of farm country on the L and 1998 ice storm damage become continual.

At a small hemlock grove at 1.5 mi, the trail forks R, uphill, at a T. The ascent is steady through significant storm damage, and the trail passes a small rock outcrop on the R at 1.8 mi as it winds uphill to a jct. with the Split Rock Mt. Trail at 2.0 mi. The L fork goes 0.2 mi to a lookout, and the R fork heads over the mountain for 2.6 mi, back to the start of the Blue Trail and then to the trailhead parking lot.

❋ Trail in winter: This old road is suitable for skiing or snowshoeing, though the hill at the N end can be arduous.

⚚ Distances: Split Rock Mt. North Rim Trail (trail 7) to old logging clearing, 0.5 mi; to fork R, 1.0 mi; to hemlock grove fork, 1.5 mi; to jct. with Split Rock Mt. North Rim Trail, 2.0 mi (3.2 km) (2.7 mi/4.3 km from trailhead via Louis Clearing Bay Trail and Split Rock Mt. North Rim Trail).

(9) Louis Clearing Bay Trail

Trails Illustrated Map #742: AA33

THE MAIN ACCESS TRAIL, marked by orange snowmobile trail disks, leads E into the woods from the parking lot (see above) (0.0 mi), heading gradually uphill on an old rutted road. At 0.1 mi another spur called "Gary's Elbow" on the trailhead map and marked blue cuts off to the R (S). (This spur to the R is a slightly longer route that rejoins the main trail at 0.8 mi.) The main trail continues on straight ahead and uphill. At 0.3 mi there is another jct. with a yellow-marked trail cutting off to the L (N), to trails 7 and 8.

Continuing straight ahead, the mostly level trail meanders through a mixed coniferous and deciduous forest, crossing over a couple of streams. At 0.7 mi, it passes a wet area with a water hole on the L and soon climbs gradually and swings around to the L. After it levels off again, Gary's Elbow (trail 9A) comes in from the R at a Y at 0.8 mi. The main trail gradually begins descending and at 1.0 mi the start of the Barn Rock Trail (10) is on the R (S).

The trail continues straight ahead, following a series of hemlock-covered ledges on the L with a number of sturdy old grapevines hanging from the trees along the trail. After dropping steadily for a while, the trail levels and Lake Champlain can be seen shining through the trees in the distance.

At an intersection at 1.4 mi, the Louis Clearing Bay Trail heads off to the L. Bearing R, in a short distance the Snake Den Bay lookout spur turns L onto a small ridge and fades to a small footpath at the height of the ridge at 1.6 mi. From there it is a short scramble down to a nice outlook through the junipers down to the Palisades on Lake Champlain with the shimmering waters of Snake Den Bay about 300 ft below.

Leaving the above jct. the trail heads N, then E down a moderately steep grade. The trail is rocky and a bit wet in a couple of places along its descent to the rocky bay. There are great views to the N, S, and E across the lake to Vermont. Descent from the Snake Den Lookout Spur is approx. 300 ft. Total ascent from Lake Champlain back to the parking lot is about 465 ft.

✳ Trail in winter: This old road is suitable for skiing or snowshoeing, with gradual grades, until it narrows to a footpath near its end.

🐾 Distances: Trailhead to water hole, 0.7 mi; to Barn Rock Trail (trail 10), 1.0 mi; to Snake Den Bay lookout spur, 1.4 mi; to lakeshore, 1.7 mi (2.7 km).

(9A) Gary's Elbow Trail

Trails Illustrated Map #742: AA33

THIS TRAIL IS A SIDEHILL RAMBLE that twice connects to and parallels the Louis Clearing Bay Trail, offering a short loop option to that hike. It is unsigned, but marked with blue disks and is 0.8 mi (1.3 km) long. The N end of the Crossover Trail (10A) connects with this nice trail also. It is fine for skiing and snowshoeing.

(10) Barn Rock Trail

Trails Illustrated Map #742: AA33

THIS YELLOW-MARKED TRAIL travels through a nice forest of mixed woods, descending to the shore of Lake Champlain and a quite unique viewpoint over the lake. It is at present unmarked and unmaintained, and is quite wet in some spots as it follows what appears to be an old carriage road to the shore of Lake Champlain. If following the overgrown trail near the end proves to be too much of a problem, following the stream will bring you down to the small isolated bay beside Barn Rock.

The trail begins (0.0 mi) at a sharp R turn at 1.0 mi on the Louis Clearing Bay Trail (trail 9) at the head of a small ravine. The trail soon veers L and climbs gradually up the side of the slope. At 0.2 mi the trail levels off, turns and heads in a S and SE direction, then gradually begins descending to a level area at 0.6 mi. The road is level with a couple of wet areas until at 0.9 mi it begins descending again.

Dropping fairly steeply at first over rocks, the trail soon changes to a more moderate descent. At 1.1 mi a beautiful old stone bridge crosses over the stream to the R to the Calamity Trail (trail 6), which leads back to Lake Shore Rd. at a point 0.8 mi S of the trailhead parking lot. The trail on the L stream bank is faint here, but follows down along some interesting rock work in the stream bed, crossing over the stream at 1.2 mi. Soon a rock wall is passed on the R, and the bay is visible through the trees with Barn Rock just beyond jutting out into Lake Champlain. A herd path cuts down the steep bank to the L and heads across the sandy shore of the small bay, while the trail itself continues on for a short distance, ending at 1.5 mi at a small stream where beaver activity may be in evidence.

If Barn Rock is the only goal, then the herd path down the steep bank would be the shortest route. Going to the end of the trail, however, gives a nice perspective of Barn Rock and the beaver work in the area, and it's a nice short walk back along the shoreline to the herd path up to Barn Rock. Follow the cobbled shoreline back a short distance and then cross the short gravelly section at the mouth of the bay. Head R (E) along the shoreline toward Barn Rock to a small gully on the L. This is the easiest herd path ascent up to the top of the ridge. Follow up the L side of the gully and then turn R along the herd path along the center of the ridge. The main path soon heads over to the R side, then back to the center again before arriving at the end of Barn Rock, with beautiful views along and across Lake Champlain. Keep an eye out for Champ, the famous Lake Champlain creature! Distance from the trail at the bay is approx. 0.4 mi, or 1.9 mi from the Louis Clearing Bay Trail (trail 9).

❋ Trail in winter: At first a gradual and finally a steep descent to the lake, then a long climb back up; great for skis and snowshoes!

❋ Distances: Louis Clearing Bay Trail to stone bridge, 1.1 mi; to end of trail along shore, 1.5 mi; to end of Barn Rock, 1.9 mi (3.1 km) (2.9 mi/4.7 km from parking lot). Descent to the lake from the highest point on the trail, approx. 510 ft.

(10A) **Crossover Trail**

Trails Illustrated Map #742: AA32–33
THIS NEW (2008) YELLOW-MARKED TRAIL runs N-S, connecting the Calamity Trail and the Gary's Elbow spur trail (9A), making possible a loop between the S end of the trail system and the main trailhead.

The trail generally contours along a hillside, descends to cross a brook and ascends steeply to its intersection with the blue-marked

Gary's Elbow spur trail. Its length is approximately one mile (1.6 km) and is most suitable in winter for snowshoes (more detailed description to follow in future revisions of this guidebook).

(11) Coon Mt. Preserve

Trails Illustrated Map #742: AA32

The Coon Mt. Preserve is a 246-acre property located in the Adirondack Land Trust's Champlain Valley Farm and Forest Project area. The mountain includes many steep rock faces, small wetlands, and several streams, and the mixed hardwood forest supports a variety of wildlife. From the top are fine views of Lake Champlain, the Green Mountains, and the Adirondack High Peaks rising beyond the farmlands in the valley. The preserve contains most of the higher part of the mountain, and is bordered on all sides by private lands, so be sure to keep your bearings straight to avoid becoming lost and wandering onto private property.

This is a preserve. No camping, fires, or littering is allowed, nor the destruction or removal of any plants. For more up-to-date information please call the Adirondack Nature Conservancy and Adirondack Land Trust at 518-576-2082.

▶ Trailhead: Heading E on 9N from Exit 31 on the Northway (I-87), in a short distance take the L (N) turn onto Youngs Rd. (0.0 mi). Just past a R at a T intersection, the hamlet of Wadhams and the intersection with NY 22 are at 2.6 mi. Continue L (N and E) on NY 22, taking the R turn (SE) onto Morrison Rd. at 3.7 mi. In another mi, cross the RR tracks and bridge over the Boquet River. Bear R, then cross the road that parallels the river onto Halds Rd., which soon enters a wooded area. There is a small parking lot by the road on the L (N) side at 5.5 mi, by the Adirondack Land Trust signs. ◀

THE TRAIL LEAVES the N end of the parking lot (0.0 mi) on the level to a green and white trail sign at 0.1 mi and bears L uphill. It passes through a hemlock and beech woods on a sidehill. The summit rocks are visible up to the L through the trees.

The trail becomes rocky and steeper as it starts up into a ravine at 0.4 mi. At 0.6 mi it reaches a T fork at the base of a rock face. The fork L goes 20 yd to a nice lookout over Northwest Bay of Lake Champlain. Be careful of the drop-off!

The trail continues N over many rocks up the W side of the ravine, to its head at a trail sign at 0.8 mi. It levels off going W past a vernal pool on stepping stones in a small notch.

The trail rises S along a lichen-encrusted rock face through pines and oaks. It briefly switches back onto itself and up onto the summit at 1.0 mi. There are two lookouts: one to the W of the High Peaks with farm country in the foreground, and the higher one to the S and E across the lake to the Green Mountains in Vermont.

RICHARD NOWICKI

❋ Trail in winter: Suitable for snowshoeing but not skiing, due to its steep middle section.

🐾 Distances: Parking lot to T fork at base of cliff, 0.6 mi; to summit, 1.0 mi (1.6 km). Summit elevation, 1015 ft (308 m).

(11A) Hidden Valley Trail

Trails Illustrated Map #742: AA32

▶ Trailhead: See trail 11. ◀

THIS TRAIL LEAVES the parking lot (0.0 mi) on the L and follows an old logging road for 0.2 mi uphill and then down. At a trail sign with an arrow pointing R, the trail leaves the woods road, zigzagging downhill to two sets of stepping stones over small wet spots. At a second wooden direction sign which points R at 0.5 mi, the trail climbs again. Two sets of cliffs are on the L, and then the trail passes between two small rocky knolls before it meet the Coon Mt. trail (trail 11) at 0.8 mi. The trailhead is reached by turning R, downhill, completing the loop at 1.0 mi.

✴ Trail in winter: Suitable for snowshoeing, but too tight for skiing.

𝕸 Distances: Parking lot to first wooden sign, 0.2 mi; to second wooden sign, 0.5 mi; to parking lot, 1.0 mi (1.6 km).

(11B) Little Falls Preserve

Trails Illustrated Map #742: AA31–32

This 15-acre preserve along the Bouquet River is owned by the Adirondack Conservancy and Land Trust and is open for picnicking, swimming, and is a good canoe put-in spot above or below the falls. It would be a nice spot to swim on a hot day after a hike up Coon Mt., which is less than a three-mile drive away. This is a popular spot for local swimmers.

▶ Trailhead/Parking: Access is E on the Merriam Forge Rd., which is located just off NY 22, 2.2 mi N of the hamlet of Wadhams in the town of Westport. A parking pull-off spot is at the bend just across the RR tracks on the N side of the road, and a path leads N 300 yd along the tracks to a pretty rocky point above the falls and the river. ◀

FOUR PONDS

Trails Illustrated Map #742: X30

While there are a couple of short trails in and around these ponds, more have been added to round out the experience in this region along Essex County Rte. 7, the Lincoln Pond Rd. A day in the area might include some canoeing and swimming or fishing on the ponds and a short hike up Belfry Mt. for some fine views. In winter, a pleasant ski or snowshoe loop could be done through all four of these ponds.

▶ Trailheads: Just E of Exit 30 on the Adirondack Northway (I-87), take the first L onto the Mineville Rd. (Essex Co. Rte. 6) and follow this to the first intersection in Witherbee. Turn L (0.0 mi) onto Essex Co. Rte. 70, Dalton Hill Rd., toward Belfry Mt. and Lincoln Pond. At 1.3 mi, Rte. 7C joins Rte. 7 at a Y; this is Lincoln Pond Rd. Continue L; at 1.6 mi a dirt road to the R (N) leads to both Tanaher (12) and Mill (13) ponds. At 1.8 mi, another dirt road R leads to the W end of Mill Pond and is near Murrey Pond (14). On the R at 2.0 mi is the footpath to Russett Pond (15), the last in this series of ponds. From this point it is about 2.3 mi N on Rte. 7 to the Lincoln Pond state campground. ◀

(12) **Tanaher Pond**

Trails Illustrated Map #742: X30

THIS IS A PRETTY POND, ringed with a boggy shoreline. From the road (see trailhead description above), drive downhill about 125 yd to a Y. Bear R (E) for a short distance to a pull-off at 0.1 mi. From there the pond is visible and there's a short wet path (N) leading to the edge of the pond at 0.2 mi (0.3 km).

(13) **Mill Pond**

Trails Illustrated Map #742: X30

THE TRAIL STARTS at the same access as for Tanaher Pond (12). Heading downhill on the dirt road to the Y at 125 yd, bear L (W). The road soon dissipates into an unmarked footpath that wanders over a couple of knolls and down to a small access at the shoreline of Mill Pond at 0.2 mi (0.3 km).

(14) **Murrey Pond**

Trails Illustrated Map #742: X30

THIS IS A SHORT, moderately steep access to both the SW corner of Mill Pond and to Murrey Pond. From the road (see trailhead above), a dirt road leads a short distance down the hill, with a couple of footpaths leading to the water at 0.1 mi (0.2 km).

(15) **Russett Pond**

Trails Illustrated Map #742: X30

THIS IS THE CLOSEST POND to the road. It's only about 50 yd along the footpath to the pond from the parking along the shoulder of the road by the Forest Preserve sign (see trailhead above).

(16) **Belfry Mt.**

Trails Illustrated Map #742: X30

THIS IS A REAL TREAT: a short walk and a fantastic view, the lazy hiker's heaven. High Peaks Audubon members come up here to watch hawks fly low over this peak during their fall and spring migrations. At other times it is possible to see a few hawks soaring, so bring your binoculars.

▶ Trailhead: In Mineville, turn L between the Rexall drug store and Citgo gas station. Drive 1.0 mi to a yield sign. Turn R on County Rte. 7C where a brown sign says "Elizabethtown 11, Lincoln Pond 4." Go 1.1 mi uphill. Park on the shoulder of the road on the R, across from a bright yellow steel gate on the L (0 mi). There is a trailhead sign with red markers next to the gate. Be sure to park outside the gate, which gets locked daily. The top of the hill by the gate is 3.5 mi SE of the Lincoln Pond state campground and day-use area. ◀

FROM THE GATE (0.0 mi), the route follows the ranger access road 0.2 mi to a cabin and radio tower, then at 0.3 mi reaches a clearing and two sheds. The fire tower is in sight. At just under 0.4 mi the trail achieves the summit.

From the fire tower, which can be climbed, there are good views of Lake Champlain, Vermont to the E, the Dix Range to the W, the Great Range, Whiteface to the NW, Rocky Peak Ridge, Giant, and Hurricane Mt. to the N. Mineville and the slag heaps left over from the days of the iron mines can be seen below.

✳ Trail in winter: Suitable for a short ski or snowshoe trip.

𝕸 Distance: Road to summit, 0.4 mi (0.6 km). Ascent, 120 ft (36 m). Summit elevation, 1820 ft (558 m).

(17) Morehouse Bridge to Boquet

Trails Illustrated Map #742: CC32

This is a pleasant and easy walk along an old road that starts in the Town of Willsboro and ends in the Town of Essex. Take along a picnic and eat lunch on the ledges of the Boquet River. This is an excellent mountain bike or cross-country ski route. The road has been abandoned by the towns, but access is legal, even past the new camp near its S end.

▶ Trailhead: From Essex, go W on NY 22 1.5 mi to the Middle Road. Turn R (N) and go 1.8 mi to Coonrod Rd. Turn L (W) and go 1.7 mi to Morehouse Bridge over the Boquet River. Cross the bridge and at 1.8 mi turn L onto a dirt road which ends at the old McAuliffe farm. Be sure to park on the grassy beyond the barn where you are not blocking the driveways—the school bus turns around here. ◀

THE HIKE STARTS from the farm, straight ahead through fields on the abandoned road. At 0.1 mi, the road passes a pond down to the L, then starts going gently uphill, at 0.3 mi gently downhill, then uphill again. At 0.4 mi the road enters woods; soon there is an old clearing on the R and a junked refrigerator. The road descends.

At 0.5 mi the road curves L high over a stream, then uphill and into a sunny field on the R. North Boquet Mt. is visible across the field. At 0.6 mi the road reenters woods and at 0.7 mi reaches the end of the field, seen through the trees. Now the road goes gradually downhill. At 0.8 mi the river can be heard down to the L.

The road goes gently uphill and then down again. At 1.0 mi there is a rock ledge on the R, then a muddy and overgrown field and at 1.1 mi the abandoned clubhouse of the Boquet Snowdrifters, a snowmobile club, at the Willsboro-Essex town line.

At 1.2 mi the road crosses a stream on a broken bridge. A side track L leads to the river. Now the road goes uphill past a huge rock ledge on the L, covered with ferns and mosses, and across a flat.

At 1.3 mi there is a turn-out and small new camp on the L above the river, from which the river can be seen and heard down the steep hill on the L. At 1.5 mi a paved road goes up Crooked S Hill. A walk downhill L to another track on the L in 200 ft leads to an easy path to the shelving ledges and waterfall at 1.6 mi, below a bridge over the river. Across the river are the remains of a stone mill, one of several that were here in the little hamlet of Boquet more than 100 years ago. Now this is a popular local picnic, fishing, and swimming spot.

❋ Trail in winter: Suitable for gentle skiing and snowshoeing.

ᴍ Distances: McAuliffe farm to abandoned clubhouse, 1.1 mi; to Crooked S Hill, 1.5 mi; to Boquet River ledges, 1.6 mi (2.6 km).   ◆

View from Mt. Gilligan. NANCIE BATTAGLIA

Hammond Pond Wild Forest, Crown Point, Moriah Section

This section is centrally located within the eastern Adirondack region. It's bordered by Elizabethtown, Mineville, and Port Henry on the N, and NY 74 from Exit 28 on the Northway (I-87) to Ticonderoga on the S. The E side is a pretty landscape of farmlands along Lake Champlain, while the W side is the extensive Hammond Pond Wild Forest area that is bounded by US 9 on the W. This region underwent extensive review in the late 1980s and most of the suggested improvements have taken place. At present the area sees little use, especially when compared to the Pharaoh Lake Wilderness just to the S. While a trail system connects some of the most popular destinations, several trailless mountains and isolated ponds wait to be explored. The Hammond Pond Wild Forest area is perfect for an ultralight "Lost Pond" boat.

❋ Trails in winter: Most of the marked trails in this region are over low rolling terrain and are perfect for skiing and snowshoeing. Other recommendations for specific trails are listed with the trail descriptions.

Suggested hikes in the region include:

SHORT HIKE:
• Arnold Pond—0.3 mi (0.5 km). A short but steep hike to a pretty pond tucked in at the base of a rock slide on Skiff Mt.

MODERATE HIKE:
• Peaked Hill—2.2 mi (3.5 km) plus canoe. This is a fun summer route, canoeing across Paradox Lake and then hiking a moderate route to Peaked Hill Pond followed by the steeper climb up Peaked Hill.

HARDER HIKE:
• Sharp Bridge Campground to Round Pond and East Mill Flow— 10.4 mi (16.8 km) round trip. Rolling woods and wetlands to a pretty pond.

(17A) **Black Kettle Nature Trail**

Trails illustrated Map #742: BB32

This interesting trail is on the land of Black Kettle Farm in Whallonsburgh and owned by the Eddy Foundation. The Foundation is working to protect lands in the Champlain Valley in order to create a wildlife corridor from Forest Preserve lands at Split Rock Mt. (trails 6–10) along the Lake, to protected lands in the High Peaks further west. Achievement of this aim before the valley becomes more developed will avoid isolation of the wildlife populations along the lakeshore; they will then be able to travel back and forth for their food, habitat, and mating needs, thus ensuring survival. The trail has numbered stops keyed to the text of an interpretive flyer that is available at the farm.

▶ Trailhead: From Exit 31 on I-87 (the Adirondack Northway), go

L on Youngs Rd., which is E of the overpass. Drive 2.5 mi to the intersection with Cty. Rte. 8. Turn R down the hill into Wadhams at NY Rte. 22. Continue N on NY 22 for 3.9 mi. Turn L on Cook Rd. and follow it to the red barn of Black Kettle Farm at 1.7 mi. ◀

Pull in L at the barn and park. The trail starts behind the barn. (Note: In late 2005, the trail work was not quite complete. A few more plank bridges were needed, but footing all the way was good.)

THE TRAIL LEAVES the back of the barn and crosses a small stream in the clearing and then heads uphill to a red and black trail sign at the edge of the woods. The trail is marked with white plastic butterfly-shaped markers. Cross the first of many downed logs, winding uphill past large pines and hemlocks. The trail is on a side hill and also goes under several partly downed trees before skirting a small clearing covered with Reindeer Moss and with views to the E. Avoid the temptation of walking on the moss, and stay on the trail in the woods. Much of it is on a side-hill, before it descends steeply to a stream crossing at 0.3 mi. Cross the brook and several small plank bridges on the far side, until an old woods road is reached. Walk L along the old road, downhill, until the trail veers off L to a wetland. Skirt the wetland, and eventually cross it on more planks. Then the barn is in sight, and walk up through the field to the trail's end at 0.6 mi.

🐾 Distances: Barn to stream crossing, 0.3 mi (0.5 km); back to barn, 0.6 mi (1.0 km).

(18) Sunrise Trail to Mt. Gilligan

Trails Illustrated Map #742: Y28

Formerly known as Sunrise Mt., this little peak rises directly above the Boquet River and offers views of Pleasant Valley, Rocky Peak Ridge, and the Dixes from the summit and the several lookouts along the way. This hike is entirely on private land; please respect the privilege of access.

▶ Trailhead: The trail starts from US 9, 3.6 mi N of its jct. with NY 73 and 2.6 mi S of the New Russia Post Office. A dirt road E leads to a bridge over the river, with an informal parking lot just before the bridge. Park here (0.0 mi), cross the bridge, and turn L off the road after 150 yd, just before reaching a house on the L. Marked sporadically with ADK markers and red disks, the well-maintained trail proceeds on the flat for a few hundred yards before climbing to a higher shelf up to the R and then, after some more flat going, climbs steeply up to the first lookout at 0.3 mi, with a good view of Dix. ◀

CONTINUING ON, the trail dips briefly and then climbs steadily to another lookout at 0.6 mi. Now the grade is easier along the top of the ridge before the trail dips down and crosses an old lumber road in a small col at 0.8 mi. Climbing past an interesting overhung rock, the trail reaches a broad open area after approx. 100 yd, with good views of Rocky Peak Ridge and the Dix Range. Just after this ledge, the trail joins and briefly follows an old lumber road before branching L and up to the final lookout at 1.1 mi at the end of the trail. The wooded summit of Gilligan Mt. is about 100 yd beyond.

᠉ Distances: Parking area to first lookout, 0.3 mi; to second lookout, 0.6 mi; to lookout below summit of Mt. Gilligan, 1.1 mi (1.8 km). Ascent, 670 ft (204 m). Elevation, 1420 ft (433 m).

(19) **Bald Peak**

Trails Illustrated Map #742: Y28

This is a rewarding climb that is technically part of the High Peaks region and part of the much longer Rocky Peak Ridge trail. Much of the trail is in the open, and there are views all along the way. Be sure, though, to bring plenty of water on a hot summer day, and crampons in the winter for the exposed upper reaches of Bald Peak. On a cool fall day with Adirondack colors at their peak, this is a spectacular hike. Except for a small stand of first-growth hemlock near the start of the trail, this entire route is through smaller second growth. This is a result of the great fire of 1913, which burned all of Rocky Peak and much of adjacent Giant. Nearly all of the views along this route are a result of this last major fire in the Adirondacks; these views encompass most of the area covered by this book.

▶ Trailhead: The trail begins at a parking lot on the W side of US 9, 4.9 mi N of its jct. with NY 73 and 1.3 mi S of the New Russia Post Office. ◀

FROM THE PARKING LOT the yellow-marked trail crosses a nearly grown-up field, begins to climb an old tote road, and comes to the L bank of a small stream at 0.7 mi. Following up the L bank, the trail enters a flat notch, at the far end of which it swings L and climbs to the first view on the L at 1.6 mi. A second view is just off the trail to the R at 1.8 mi.

Continuing up, the trail comes to the first lookout on Blueberry Cobbles on the L at 1.9 mi and then reaches a jct. at 2.0 mi with a red trail leading R that bypasses the top of Blueberry Cobbles. (In season there is no doubt that Blueberry Cobbles is appropriately named.) The yellow trail L leads past many other views of the Boquet Valley and the Dix Range before turning sharp R and down at 2.3 mi to Mason Notch, where the red bypass trail rejoins it. The trail climbs over the slightly wooded summit of Mason Mt. (2330 ft) at 2.8 mi before descending to Hedgehog Notch at the base of Bald Peak.

Now the trail begins to climb steeply over mostly bare rock to the summit of Bald Peak (3060 ft) at 3.9 mi, where there are good views in all directions. From the summit one can look out over most of the eastern Adirondack region, as well as some of the High Peaks region. Further hiking possibilities in the High Peaks region are described in ADK's *Adirondack Trails: High Peaks Region.*

❋ Trail in winter: This trail is not a skiing route, but makes a great snowshoeing trail. With poor snow conditions, crampons (full or instep) are a must for the steeper exposed sections.

🐾 Distances: Parking lot to stream, 0.7 mi; to Blueberry Cobbles, 1.9 mi; to Mason Mt. summit, 2.8 mi; to top of Bald Peak, 3.9 mi (6.3 km). Ascent, 2447 ft (746 m). Elevation, 3060 ft (933 m).

Split Rock Falls (unmarked footpaths)

Trails Illustrated Map #742: Y48

Currently there is no marked trail system in the Split Rock Falls area, but several herd paths lead around the falls, along the river, and to the base of the falls, a popular swimming spot on a hot summer day. Several well-built woods roads to the S and W of the falls make excellent cross-country ski trails as they wind up the side of Split Rock Mountain.

With the addition of a parcel of land surrounding the falls to the Forest Preserve, there is potential for marked trails in the region in the future. Unfortunately, a fair amount of trash is left in the vicinity by careless visitors. Extreme care should be exercised in proximity to the falls.

▶ Trailhead: The parking lot is along the E side of US 9, 2.3 mi N of NY 73 and 3.8 mi S of the New Russia Post Office. The parking lot is small and there are No Parking signs along both sides of the road for some distance beyond the parking lot, so on a hot summer day it may be necessary to walk some distance to get to the falls ◀.

A COUPLE OF HERD PATHS and woods roads lead E from the parking lot along the edge of the gorge, with a couple more heading down the steep sides to the Boquet River and the base of the multi-stage falls. It can be fun to explore downstream along the river as well. Another footpath leads along the river from the S side of the bridge across the Boquet River. This also leads downstream along the falls and to the river. The falls is a very pretty spot, as is the area downstream, where the steep rocky sides become gradually narrower along the riverbanks. There is an informal campsite on the E side of the river between the two main sets of falls.

A third of a mile W of the falls, on US 9, is a Forest Preserve sign at a woods road whose entrance is blocked by boulders. This road can be used as the start of a ski exploration of this area, or as an easy bush-whack hike up Split Rock Mt., which overlooks the falls. Be sure to stay on state land upon reaching Posted signs at the top of the ridge.

(21) (Proposed)

Trail 21 is a proposed trail within the vicinity. A description will be added in the next edition of this guide.

(22) Crowfoot Pond

Trails Illustrated Map #742: W29

This old road is a very pleasant walk in the fall. The trees are spectacular and the brook becomes an old friend as you cross and recross it three times before reaching the pond. It is also an excellent cross-country ski run. All of the bridges across Crowfoot Brook are ramped for snowmobiles. It might be good to inquire locally about the frequency of snowmobile use because this used to be a designated snowmobile trail.

▶ Trailhead: At Northway (I-87) Exit 30, drive E on US 9 and make an immediate L turn onto Tracy Rd., just after the northbound Northway entrance ramp. Go 1.8 mi down this curving road to a track forking off to the R. This used to be a town road. Park on the shoulder of Tracy Rd. or in the clearing just off the road. ◀

FROM THE START on Tracy Rd. (0.0 mi), yellow trail signs on a dead tree can be seen 50 ft down the old road. The road follows Crowfoot Brook on the R, past a Forest Preserve sign on a tree on the R, and at 0.1 mi crosses a bridge over Crowfoot Brook. After the bridge, the trail turns L and climbs gently through hemlocks and birches. The road now traverses a hill high above the brook.

At 0.3 mi, the road crosses two water bars at a spring. The woods now are more deciduous with many ferns along the path.

At 0.5 mi, the trail bends L and R again around a small, fern-lined streambed. Then it enters darker woods with more hemlocks, as it passes a small stone wall on the R.

At 0.8 mi there is another bridge over Crowfoot Brook. The road now climbs steadily upward. At 1.1 mi it begins to descend, and at 1.3 mi crosses another log bridge. At 1.7 mi, the road recrosses the brook, then a smaller streambed, then at 2.0 mi, a bridge. At 2.1 mi, a Forest Preserve marker is on the L in a rock cairn.

At 2.3 mi, the road divides in a small clearing. Continue straight through the clearing, not on the R track. At 2.5 mi, the W end of Crowfoot Pond comes into view. At 2.7 mi, there is a log cabin camp on a hillside on the L, then another camp, then about 10 more camps farther E on the pond. The road runs along the shoreline, with a lovely view of the wooded hill across the long narrow pond.

At 3.0 mi the road reaches the end of public land at a "POSTED" sign; beyond is not a public right of way.

✻ Trail in winter: Excellent for skiing or snowshoeing.

𝕸 Distance: Tracy Rd. to second bridge, 0.8 mi; to rock cairn, 2.1 mi; to Crowfoot Pond, 3.0 mi (4.8 km).

(23) Sharp Bridge Campground to Round Pond and East Mill

Trails Illustrated Map #742: W28

This trail is a relatively flat and pleasant walk through some fine woods, giving access to picturesque Round Pond as well as the beautiful and unique open area known as East Mill Flow. This trail was cut out a few years ago but has not been well maintained recently. It is still quite passable, though; one only needs to be careful not to lose it in the alders at a few of the stream crossings.

▶ Trailhead: The start is at Sharp Bridge Campground on Rte. 9, 7.1

mi N of the village of North Hudson and 2.9 mi S of Exit 30 on the Adirondack Northway (I-87). Parking is at the gravel turnout just outside the gate. ◀

FROM THE PARKING AREA (0.0 mi), the trail goes to the far end of the large, flat field near the Schroon River and then along the L bank of the river on an old road. Crossing several small brooks, the trail comes to an old bridge abutment at 0.8 mi. This apparently was the original crossing point used as early as the 1830s by both the predecessor of US 9 and by a road leading W from Port Henry to Tahawus and beyond. Turning sharp L at this point, the trail follows this old road for several miles.

The trail climbs briefly, drops to cross a small brook, and then begins a steady climb to a height of land at 1.5 mi. Dropping down the other side in two short pitches, the trail continues mostly on the level through several magnificent stands of white pine to the R bank of East Mill Brook at 2.7 mi, at the S end of East Mill Flow.

Swinging R, the trail drops down and makes a somewhat difficult crossing of the brook before scrambling up the far bank and continuing along the E side of this extensive open swamp. At 3.4 mi, the trail crosses the outlet to Round Pond in a thick clump of alders, turns sharp R, and heads up a gentle grade. At 3.5 mi, just before coming within sight of Round Pond, the trail turns sharp R off the old road and proceeds to the outlet of Round Pond at 3.9 mi. (The old road leads straight ahead to the NW shore of Round Pond with a good campsite located across the pond on some low rocks.)

From the outlet, the trail climbs S away from the pond and skirts numerous small swampy areas as it crosses a low divide and proceeds down to a jct. with an unmarked trail leading L at 4.5 mi. (The trail L leads along E shore of Trout Pond to a rough access road.) Continuing R, the trail makes its way along the W shore of Trout Pond and comes to the North Hudson–Moriah Rd. at 5.2 mi. This trailhead is approx. 6.2 mi from US 9, N of North Hudson.

🏔 Distances: Sharp Bridge Campground to old bridge abutment, 0.8 mi; to height of land, 1.5 mi; to East Mill Flow, 2.7 mi; to outlet of Round Pond, 3.9 mi; to North Hudson–Moriah Rd., 5.2 mi (8.4 km).

(24) **Howard and Munson Ponds**

Trails Illustrated Map #742: W28

These are two jewel-like ponds along the Moriah Rd. in the Town of North Hudson.

▶Trailhead: Drive 2.4 mi N from North Hudson on US 9 to a R (NE) on Rte. 4, known locally as the Moriah Rd. A sign here indicates the way to Port Henry. Drive 5.7 mi E from NY 9 on Rte. 4, the Moriah Rd. Park at a turn-out on the R, just before an interesting and historic white stone marker which delineates the boundary between the towns of Moriah and North Hudson. Walk back W along the road 100 ft to a huge pair of white pines until you come to the marshy opening of the path on the L (N) side of the road. There are no signs or markers, and the beginning of the trail may be a little tricky to spot. ◀

DESPITE A WET BEGINNING, the path is mostly dry, first going W parallel to the county road and then at 0.1 mi turning N and uphill within earshot of a stream. It levels at 0.2 mi along a stream with a steep hillside to the R. The path goes up again and at 0.3 mi Howard Pond can be seen. A sign (2004) says these are Special Brook Trout Waters.

At 0.4 mi, the route reaches the edge of Howard Pond. Retracing your steps 100 ft, follow a faint path to the L at the height of land just before the pond edge; it goes through a beautiful cedar and hemlock forest along the E side of the pond.

At 0.6 mi, the route passes a large white pine with a fire circle by the edge of the pond. At 0.7 mi, it leaves the NE edge of the pond and starts uphill, soon going through a large stand of maidenhair fern. It ascends steeply, at 0.9 mi reaching the top of a ridge. On the short descent the path is faint. After a slight rise, it goes downhill to a tiny, swampy pond.

At 1.0 mi, the path starts heading more steeply downhill. At 1.1 mi, Munson Pond can be seen through the trees, and in a few hundred yards it is attained. The beavers have been doing heavy-duty logging here, felling large birches around the perimeter of the pond. The pond level has been raised considerably. Although there is no formal path around this pond, it is not difficult to thread your way among the hemlocks, white pines, and birches, since their canopy is quite high.

❋ Trail in winter: Suitable for snowshoeing, but too narrow for skiing.

🏃 Distances: Moriah Rd. to Howard Pond, 0.4 mi; to Munson Pond, 1.2 mi (1.9 km).

HAMMOND POND WILD FOREST, CROWN POINT, MORIAH SECTION

(25) **Bass Lake Trail**

Trails Illustrated Map #743: V27

This is the first body of water among the family of ponds along the Moriah Rd. These ponds all feed the Schroon River to the S.

▶ Trailhead: Drive 2.4 mi N from North Hudson on US 9 to a R (NE) on Rte. 4, known locally as the Moriah Rd. A sign here indicates the way to Port Henry. After this turn, go only 0.2 mi to an old paved road to the R (E). At the end of this is the trailhead with yellow markers. ◀

LEAVING THE MORIAH RD. (0.0 mi), the old paved road turns to dirt in several hundred yards at an old bridge abutment on both sides of the stream on the L. A fisherman's path goes down the steep bank to the stream. The trail passes a wide place in the stream below at 0.2 mi. Now it cuts along the bank and at 0.3 mi passes shelving falls through the trees on the L. The trail now bends R uphill and away from the stream.

At 0.4 mi, the trail levels off. Crossing a stream, it heads up steeply through birch and hemlock woods. At 0.8 mi, it crosses a small brook. At 1.0 mi, the trail, still climbing, becomes muddy, eroded and rocky. It soon levels off in a beech woods and then descends along a ridge.

At 1.4 mi, the trail turns L to avoid a blowdown, goes through a sunny area and then enters some tall hemlocks. At 1.6 mi, Bass Lake is visible through the trees, and a side trail L leads 0.2 mi to the W end of the lake by a huge boulder.

The trail continues on to the R parallel to the S shore of Bass Lake. It soon crosses a stream and then at 1.8 mi comes to another side trail that leads a short distance to an informal campsite on Bass Lake. The trail continues on along the shoreline, reaching the outlet at 2.2 mi, where there are signs of beaver activity. At 2.3 mi, it comes to the E end of the lake with nice views back across the water. After passing through a wet area, the trail levels off in open hemlocks at 2.5 mi.

The trail soon descends gradually, with Berrymill Flow visible through the trees at 2.9 mi. The trail roughly parallels the shoreline of the flow, and reaches the jct. with the Berrymill Flow and Moose Mt. Pond trail (trail 27) at 3.2 mi. From this point it is 1.4 mi to the Hammond Pond trailhead on the Moriah Rd., following the Berrymill Flow and Moose Mt. Pond trail.

❊ Trail in winter: Suitable for skiing and snowshoeing.

🐾 Distances: To first side trail to Bass Lake, 1.6 mi; to E end of lake, 2.3 mi; to Berrymill Flow and Moose Mt. Pond trail (27), 3.2 mi (5.1 km).

(26) **Challis Pond**

Trails Illustrated Map #743: V28

ADK ARCHIVES

This is another of the lovely ponds near the Moriah Rd. These are lightly traveled trails which are used mostly by trout fishermen. It would be pleasant to hike in with an inflatable raft or ultralight canoe for further exploring.

▶ Trailhead: Drive 2.4 mi N from North Hudson on US 9 to a R (NE) on Rte. 4, known locally as the Moriah Rd. A sign here indicates the way to Port Henry. At 2.6 mi (0.2 mi from US 9) is the trailhead R for Bass Lake (trail 25). At 2.7 mi, turn R again at signs for Moriah and Champlain Bridge. This is a beautiful, winding road. At 5.3 mi, park at a small turn-out R at the trailhead for Challis Pond. There might not be a sign, but someone has built a cedar railing on both sides of the trail about 50 ft up from the road. ◀

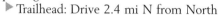

FROM THE ROAD (0.0 mi), the clearly defined trail leads up through hemlock and cedar woods. At 0.3 mi, a stream can be heard on the R but is unseen. There are orange paint blazes on trees.

At 0.4 mi, the pond's outlet stream is on the R. The trail crosses dry ground above a small seep. At 0.5 mi it enters deciduous woods; at 0.6 mi, the pond comes into view through the trees.

A campsite with a blackened boulder is near the edge of the pond. The pond seems to be almost a perfect circle. Bullfrogs call a welcome, as well as chickadees, warblers, thrushes, and nuthatches. Bog laurel, pickerel weed, and pond lilies bloom along the shoreline. There are no beavers here.

To the R, an informal path crosses the outlet stream and then continues through hemlocks around the shoreline, but peters out after 0.2 mi. This is probably used by hunters and anglers.

𝕸 Distance: Moriah Rd. to Challis Pond, 0.6 mi (1.0 km).

(27) **Berrymill Flow and Moose Mt. Pond**

Trails Illustrated Map #743: V28

This is an easy trail into some nice wild lands. There's a good opportunity to see some wildlife on the way past the flow. There's a lot of beaver activity near Moose Mt. Pond, giving a close-up look at what they can do with some fairly level drainages. Maps, including the one used as the base map for this book, identify the flow as Berrymill Pond, but trail signs, and consequently this book, refer to it as Berrymill Flow.

▶ Trailhead: Drive 2.4 mi N from North Hudson on US 9 to a R (NE) on Rte. 4, known locally as the Moriah Rd. A sign here indicates the way to Port Henry. Proceed 3.0 mi from Rte. 9 (5.4 mi from North Hudson) to a parking area on the R (S) side of the Moriah Rd. This is just 0.1 mi past the Challis Pond trailhead (trail 26). ◀

THE TRAIL BEGINS at a rustic set of steps at the S end of the parking lot (0.0 mi) and follows blue markers. It soon joins an old tote road and parallels a stream on a very gradual incline. At 0.4 mi, just before entering an open area with some substantial beaver activity, the trail cuts off to the R (W) and begins climbing a hill. It continues up and down along the hillside until descending to the old tote road again at 0.7 mi. The trail continues S along the stream through a pretty woods, reaching a 5-ft waterfall on the L (E) at 0.9 mi. It continues on at a gradual grade, reaching the jct. with the Bass Lake Trail (trail 25) at 1.4 mi. This jct. is marked with a DEC signpost.

Just beyond this jct. there is an informal campsite on a small knoll. From here is a nice view S across Berrymill Flow. After passing through the campsite, the trail crosses a bridge across the outlet of the flow, climbs a few stairs, and then begins to follow S along the shoreline of the flow. At 1.7 mi, about halfway down the flow, the trail swings L away from the flow and gradually ascends a couple of small sets of stairs. It soon meets and follows the L bank of a small stream.

At 2.1 mi, still heading E, the trail begins following an old tote road above the stream. The forest is relaxing here, with a lot of tall pines, hemlocks, poplars, and cedars. The trail soon rejoins the stream, but at 2.3 mi veers L away from the stream again. At 2.4 mi, an opening in the trees far to the L gives hope that the pond isn't too far away, but this is just an isolated wet area.

The trail soon ascends a short steep section and at 2.8 mi reaches the first of a couple of recent beaver ponds that flood the trail. It is possible to skirt the flooding through the woods on the L for a short distance.

Following along the beaver ponds, the trail is again flooded at 3.1 mi. Moose Mt. Pond isn't far away, and at 3.2 mi a spur trail to the R leads to an informal campsite with a nice view on the W shore of the pond. The trail continues E within sight of the shoreline through a pretty woods, reaching the lean-to at 3.5 mi. This is a great site with views from the shore looking across the pond to Moose Mt. and Owl Pate.

✻ Trail in winter: Suitable for skiing and snowshoeing.

🐾 Distances: Parking lot to Bass Lake Trail (trail 25), 1.4 mi; to swing away from Berrymill Flow, 1.7 mi; to Moose Mt. Pond, 3.2 mi; to lean-to, 3.5 mi (5.6 km).

(28) Hammond and Bloody Ponds

Trails Illustrated Map #743: V28

▶ Trailhead: See above, Berrymill Flow and Moose Mt. Pond (trail 27). The Hammond Pond Trail heads L (SE) from the parking lot. This is a woods road that gradually diminishes to a trail that ends at a beaver flow. ◀

FROM THE PARKING LOT (0.0 mi), the woods road crosses a sandy rise in white pines, following red markers, to a bridge at 0.1 mi on solid stone abutments. Now the route is level along the bank above the stream on the R. At 0.2 mi, the trail leaves the stream. At 0.4 mi, a swamp is visible through trees on the L. The trail, strewn with pine needles through woods of white pine, hemlock, birch, and maple, dips gently. After a stand of red pines, it continues on the level through a stand of hemlocks.

At 0.6 mi, there is a stream on the L. There is a culvert for a small feeder stream at 0.7 mi, after which the trail divides. (Uphill to the L on a 0.3-mi spur trail to a wide plank spillway at a dam, there is a good view of Blood Mt. across Hammond Pond; total distance to the pond from the trailhead is 1.0 mi. In July the deer flies are pesky, but in winter this would be a good cross-country ski destination.)

The main trail continues uphill. At 0.8 mi, Hammond Pond comes into view again, and at 0.9 mi another opening gives a view of a weedy edge of the pond. Wildlife is prolific here. On the R is a spring with a black plastic pipe as a faucet.

At 1.2 mi, there is a cement culvert over a dry brook. The trail goes along a small weed-filled pond at 1.4 mi, descending L to a broken bridge at 1.5 mi. The trail is growing in considerably. There is a stream on the R.

At 1.7 mi, another rotting bridge crosses the outlet from Bloody Pond. (To hike the 0.2 mi to Bloody Pond, turn L at a yellow paint

67

blaze on a tree after crossing the bridge. Follow the old yellow paint blazes carefully since the trail is faint and there are some blowdowns. This is a steep, rocky trail with a wonderful chimney to climb through. The pond is a tiny jewel surrounded by thick woods.) The road is interrupted at 1.9 mi by beavers at work. Since it goes onto private land soon, it is time to turn back.

✳ Trail in winter: Suitable for snowshoeing and skiing.

𝕸 Distances: To Hammond Pond spur, 0.7 mi (to Hammond Pond via spur, 1.0 mi); to Bloody Pond spur, 1.7 mi (to Bloody Pond via spur, 1.9 mi); to beaver swamp, 1.9 mi. Cumulative distance to Hammond Pond, Bloody Pond, and beaver swamp, 3.0 mi (4.8 km).

(29) Peaked Hill and Peaked Hill Pond

Trails Illustrated Map #743: S28

One of the charms of this trail is being able to combine some canoeing and hiking and then finish up with a swim at the end of a hike on a hot summer day. The trail is not heavily used, so once away from the lake you'll probably have it to yourself.

▶ Trailhead: The only public access to the lake and the trail is from the Paradox Lake State Campground boat launch. From the intersection of NY 74 and US 9, N of the hamlet of Schroon Lake, head E on NY 74, passing a canoe and fishing access site on the Schroon River on the S side of the road at 0.6 mi from US 9. A trailhead for the Pharaoh region is on the R at 4.1 mi, with the Paradox Lake State Campground on the L (N) side at 4.3 mi. The boat access site is 0.3 mi on the R along the campground road, just past the entrance gate. There is no sign for the campground once it's closed for the winter. A day-use fee is charged during the summer when the campground is operating. From the boat launch it's approx. a 0.5-mi canoe to the N across the lake, following along the point the campground is on, to the trailhead in a small bay on the N side of the lake. ◀

ON THE LAKESIDE there is a DEC trail sign for the pond and the mountain and a "No Camping" sign. Here (0.0 mi) the well-marked, blue-marked trail heads N away from the lake. Avoid going R on a side trail which leads to a private road in about 0.2 mi.

The trail climbs on a moderate grade, crossing under a major power line at 0.1 mi. It continues climbing and soon swings L up and across some boulders and through evergreens and hardwoods. At 0.3 mi, the grade levels off as the trail crosses a small mossy stream that cascades down the hillside on the L. The trail soon swings R and gently uphill through the hardwoods, roughly following the brook on the R.

At 0.4 mi, the trail levels again and meanders through the evergreens. A small rock ledge is traversed at 0.7 mi, then, after crossing a small stream, the trail heads up a small hill and through a beautiful mature evergreen forest. Peaked Hill Pond is visible through the trees at 0.9 mi as the trail soon drops to near the level of the pond. A small opening on the shoreline at 1.0 mi is identifiable with a DEC sign marked "Peaked Hill 1.1 miles." Here there is a view out across the pond, ringed with cedars, hemlock, and birch.

The trail continues around the shoreline of Peaked Hill Pond until at 1.3 mi it turns L (N) away from the pond on a very gradual climb through hardwood forest. After descending slightly, the trail winds along the side of a hemlock-covered hill and drops to cross a stream at 1.6 mi. Climbing along the L branch of the stream, the trail crosses a wet area on some rocks. Very shortly, more climbing begins through the hardwoods, first gradually, then rather steeply in a few spots. The trail turns R just below a boulder, a large glacial erratic, then turns up along a rocky streambed. It veers slightly L around the W side of a small hill at 2.0 mi. Avoid heading straight ahead toward the boulders and bottom of the cliff.

At the top of the hill, the trail levels for a short distance but soon turns R and climbs fairly steeply again up toward the mountain top. After crossing a small level area near the top, the trail leads up over a ridge of rock to the wooded summit ridge. It is a short distance R to a rocky outcrop at 2.2 mi, with views to the S. Peaked Hill Pond and then Paradox Lake are in the foreground, with Pharaoh Mt. on the L horizon, and on a clear day, Crane Mt. in the distance beyond Schroon Lake.

❋ Trail in winter: This route would be an excellent ski-shoe. Start out skiing on the campground road off NY 74, and ski across the lake to the lakeside trailhead. Good skiers might ski some of the first climb, but snowshoes would be easiest for the ascent. Once on top of the first hill it's a great ski in to the start of the serious climb up Peaked Hill. This is best on snowshoes since the trail ascends almost 700 ft in its last 0.5 mi.

🙰 Distances: Lakeside trail sign to top of first hill, 0.4 mi; to sign on Peaked Mt. Pond, 1.0 mi; to summit ascent, 1.6 mi; to summit lookout,

2.2 mi (3.5 km). Ascent from Paradox Lake to Peaked Hill Pond, 342 ft (104 m); from Peaked Hill Pond to top of Peaked Hill, 750 ft (229 m). Ascent from Paradox Lake, approx. 1100 ft (335 m). Elevation of Peaked Hill, approx. 1900 ft (579 m).

(30) Arnold Pond

Trails Illustrated Map #743: S29

▶ Trailhead: This short, very steep trail on the side of Skiff Mt. starts on the N side of NY 74, just W of Eagle Lake and only 0.1 mi E of the trailhead for Tubmill Marsh (trail 39) in the Pharaoh Lake area trail network. The trailhead for Arnold Pond is 7.9 mi E of Northway (I-87) Exit 28 (Ticonderoga–Paradox). Park in a lot just E of the trailhead on the S side of the road. The trail is marked with blue DEC disks. ◀

THE TRAIL STARTS UP THE HILL by a trail sign for Arnold Pond on the N side of the road (0.0 mi). This steep hillside has loose rock. The trail goes up through rocky woods where wild sweet peas bloom in July. At 0.1 mi there is a view to the S of Bear and Ragged mts. At 0.2 mi, the trail reaches a small col after a very steep climb with loose rock, and soon reaches the top of a ridge. At 0.3 mi, it reaches the edge of Arnold Pond.

A cairn-marked, unmaintained trail continues to the L up toward Skiff Mt. on private land. A short trail leads R down a solid rock walkway to the pond. Many dead trees ring the pond, attesting to the work of ambitious beavers. From the rocky cliffs on the N side of the pond, it is possible to hear or see a raven circling.

✳ Trail in winter: Suitable for snowshoes with crampons, but too steep and rocky for skiing.

🚶 Distance: NY 74 to Arnold Pond, 0.3 mi (0.5 km). Ascent from road, 347 ft (105.8 m). Elevation of Arnold Pond, 1300 ft (396.3 m).

(31) Old Ironville Rd.

Trails Illustrated Map #743: S29

There is not a more pleasant walk in the woods than this one. Although this road is still passable for 4WD vehicles and is sometimes used by snowmobiles, it is usually empty and quiet, perfect for walking or cross-country skiing. An abandoned town road, it starts in the Town of

Crown Point and ends in the Town of Ticonderoga. The Penfield Museum, consisting of several old white frame buildings, is in the center of Ironville; detailed collections regarding early local mining and power generation make it a wonderful half-day destination to combine with this hike. It is open in the summer months and in the fall for a superb Apple Festival.

▶ Trailhead: From Chilson on NY 74, drive N 4.5 mi on Corduroy Rd. to the Penfield Museum in Ironville. ◀

FROM THE PENFIELD MUSEUM (0.0 mi) the route proceeds E along the road and then turns R downhill onto Peasley Rd. At 0.1 mi there is a bridge over a series of cascades on Putnam Creek, the outlet of Penfield Pond.

At 0.2 mi, the road splits. Park here on the shoulder. Go R past a house, after which the road narrows and goes into deep woods. There are stone walls on both sides. At 0.4 mi, the road splits again; stay straight, not R. The road comes to the top of a hill, then begins to go downhill. It crosses a culvert at 0.6 mi with a large corner of a stone wall on the L. There is another side road R at 0.7 mi, followed soon by an ascent.

After an old farm clearing, there is a small stream on the R at 0.9 mi, which the route crosses shortly after. The going gets steeper, then levels out at 1.0 mi. At 1.1 mi, the road enters a stand of large hemlocks and white pine. It goes uphill again at 1.2 mi, through a clearing at 1.3 mi, and continues uphill past old stone walls. At 1.4 mi, another old road enters on the R.

At 1.5 mi there is a 5-ft-high iron post on the L (probably marking the town line between Crown Point and Ticonderoga). The road passes another old farm clearing at a height of land, and then another clearing with an old apple tree at 1.6 mi, just before another old road on the R.

Now the road goes uphill again. At 1.9 mi, there is a beautiful rocky cliff L. Past the top of the hill at 2.0 mi, the road passes through another clearing. In summer, milkweed blooms and butterflies gather nectar from the fragrant flowers. The road continues nearly level, then goes uphill slightly to meet the Warner Hill Rd. at 2.3 mi. The Warner Hill Rd. is called Towner Hill Rd. in the Town of Crown Point.

✳ Trail in winter: Excellent for skiing or snowshoeing. On skis, the return trip would be mostly downhill; the elevation changes from 894 ft in Ironville to 1256 ft at Warner Hill Rd.

꽤 Distances: Penfield Museum to bridge over Putnam Creek, 0.1 mi; to clearing, 1.3 mi; to iron post, 1.5 mi; to rocky cliff, 1.9 mi; to Warner Hill Rd., 2.3 mi (3.7 km).

Northway Access Points to the Dix Wilderness Area

(Much of the following is minimally adapted from ADK's Adirondack Trails: High Peaks Region, *ed. Tony Goodwin, 13th edition.)*

WITH THE CONSTRUCTION of the Adirondack Northway (I-87) through this area in the mid-1960s came a need to provide access to the W side of this highway, since parking is of course prohibited on the highway itself. There are four points where one can easily cross under the Northway along the 10-mi stretch from North Hudson to Exit 30 near Underwood. These access routes connect with the valleys of Lindsay Brook, West Mill Brook, and Walker Brook, plus Shingletree Pond, and are described briefly below. Access to all is from US 9. All are suitable for snowshoeing; the West Mill Brook Access (trail 34) is the best suited for skiing.

Note that parking for the purpose of hiking or camping is also prohibited at all I-87 rest areas.

(32) Lindsay Brook Access

Trails Illustrated Map #742: W27–28

THIS ROUTE, marked with red markers, starts S of the Schroon River opposite Sharp Bridge Campground (see trail 23). Going up a road for 0.1 mi, the trail takes a sharp R and crosses a stream, negotiates a heavily flooded area, and continues on through a pine forest to a culvert under the Northway at 0.9 mi (1.4 km). No trail continues beyond this culvert.

(33) Shingletree Pond

Trails Illustrated Map #742: W27-28

THIS RED-MARKED TRAIL begins at Courtney Pond on US 9, 3.5 mi S of Exit 30 or 6.3 mi N of Exit 29. This point is also 3.2 mi S of the start of trail 32, above. It leaves a parking area at the N end of the pond, crosses the inlet, and travels along the W shore for 0.4 mi. It then joins a woods road, bearing R (W) toward the Northway. Do not turn L onto private property at this fork; head gently uphill to the long and somewhat spooky culvert under the Northway. The pond is immediately on the other side, at 1.1 mi (1.8 km) and has, in addition to many dead trees, other interesting wetland botany.

(34) West Mill Brook Access

Trails Illustrated Map #742: W27

THIS ROUTE BEGINS 1.6 mi S of Sharp Bridge Campground or 5.5 mi N of the village of North Hudson. There is a large wooden signpost at the start of a narrow dirt road, which leads down to West Mill Brook at 0.2 mi, where there is a good ford. (Park just before the brook on the R at times of high water.) From the ford, the road crosses an extensive, open sandy area and reaches a concrete culvert under the Northway at 0.8 mi (1.8 km). At 1.1 mi there is a parking area just before a gate controls further access along the old road leading along the R bank of West Mill Brook. This road leads approximately 2 mi farther W before turning S and becoming obscure. Bear, Buck, and Saunders mts. are all attractive trailless destinations that can be accessed from this route.

(35) Walker Brook Access

Trails Illustrated Map #743: V27

THIS ACCESS IS 3.7 MI S of Sharp Bridge Campground or 3.4 mi N of North Hudson. Just S of two houses, there is an old green metal signpost at the end of a dirt road. Go down this road for 0.3 mi and park where a poorer road bears R. Bear in mind that this is private land and that the driveway beyond 0.3 mi is not a public road.

Go R and down this poorer road, to the L bank of the Schroon River, which must be forded (difficult in high water) because a bridge has not been replaced (2004). On the far side there is a good road that is followed uphill to a flat area 0.5 mi from US 9. Bear R just beyond and cross under the Northway through a concrete culvert at 0.7 mi (1.1 km). Walker Brook is approximately 0.2 mi beyond, with an old road leading up its R (S) bank giving access to Camels Hump, Niagara, and Nipple Top mts. (the latter is not the 4620-ft High Peak, which is W of the Dix Range from here).   ◆

Aerial view of Pharaoh Lake and the southern Pharaoh Lake Wilderness. CARL HEILMAN II

Pharaoh Lake Wilderness, Schroon Lake, Ticonderoga Section

This section contains one of the best known regions in the eastern Adirondacks, the Pharaoh Lake Wilderness. This wilderness area has many lakes and ponds, hills and mountains, and a network of interconnecting trails for trips of varied duration. There are access points to the wilderness from all sides, including the Crane Pond Rd. from the NW corner and the Pharaoh Lake access road on the S central side. These roads are both in a designated wilderness area where vehicles are prohibited. While they provide easier access to the interior parts of the region, the special qualities of the wilderness character of the region will be protected by the complete closure of the roads to motorized vehicles. Both of these roads are legally closed by DEC, but access is not yet blocked (October 2004).

All bodies of water within the Pharaoh Lake Wilderness Area are trout waters with special regulations. No more than five trout may be taken per day, and the use of fish as bait is prohibited.

This section is bounded on the N by NY 74, on the E by Lake George, on the W by Schroon Lake, and on the S by NY 8. The trails on the periphery by Ticonderoga and Schroon Lake are well worth hiking to help give a broader perspective on the whole Adirondack region.

❀ Trails in winter: Snow conditions can vary considerably in the eastern Adirondacks. In years when "nor'easters" come up the Atlantic coast, there can be powder snow on the ground most of the winter. However, when the storms travel down the St. Lawrence valley, this region is on the warm side of them, and rain and ice are the result. When the snow is good, all the trails in the region are great for snowshoeing, and all those except for the mountain climbs are excellent ski routes. Specific suggestions for certain trails are included in the trail descriptions.

Suggested hikes in the region:

SHORTER HIKES:
• Gull Pond—0.5 mi (0.8 km). An easy hike to a pretty little pond with rock ledges dropping down to the water.
• Rogers Rock—1.1 mi (1.8 km). A short but quite steep climb to a great outlook over northern Lake George.

MODERATE HIKE:
• Pharaoh Mt. from Crane Pond—4.3 mi (6.9 km) from the parking lot on the wilderness perimeter. A nice moderate climb with fine views from open areas on top.

HARDER HIKE:
• Clear Pond Trail (trail 43) counterclockwise to Treadway Mt. Trail (trail 46) and back to Putnam Pond on the Grizzle Ocean Trail (trail 47)—11.5 mi (18.5 km). A loop of four ponds plus a spectacular mountain.

TRAIL DESCRIBED	TOTAL MILES *(one way)*		PAGE
(36)	Crane Pond Rd.	2.0 (3.0 km)	77
(37)	Goose Pond	0.6 (1.0 km)	78
(38)	Long Swing Trail to Crane Pond Rd.	2.8 (4.5 km)	78
(39)	Tubmill Marsh Trail	6.4 (10.2 km)	79
(39A)	Crab Pond Spur to Glidden Marsh Trail	0.4 (0.6 km)	79
(40)	Pharaoh Mt. Trail (from Crane Pond to Pharaoh Lake)	6.2 (9.9 km)	81
(40A)	Lean-to Spur Trails	0.2 (0.3 km)	81
(41)	Glidden Marsh to Pharaoh Lake	4.4 (7.0 km)	83
(42)	Otter Pond	0.3 (0.5 km)	84
(43)	Clear Pond Trail	4.0 (6.4 km)	85
(43A)	Rock Pond Spur	0.5 (0.8 km)	85
(43B)	West Clear Pond Trail	0.6 (1.0 km)	85
(43C)	Putnam Pond to Clear Pond Trail	0.6 (1.0 km)	85
(44)	Bear Pond Trail	2.8 (4.5 km)	87
(45)	Rock Pond to Lilypad Pond	1.9 (3.0 km)	88
(45A)	North Rock Pond Trail	0.8 (1.3 km)	88
(46)	Treadway Mt. Trail	2.1 (3.5 km)	89

(47)	Grizzle Ocean Trail	5.2	(8.4 km)	91
(47A)	Grizzle Ocean Circuit Trail	1.1	(1.8 km)	91
(48)	Berrymill Flow from the North	2.0	(3.2 km)	92
(48A)	Berrymill Flow from the South	3.2	(5.1 km)	93
(49)	Lost Pond	2.6	(4.3 km)	94
(50)	Pharaoh Lake via Mill Brook	2.5	(4.0 km)	95
(51)	East Shore of Pharaoh Lake	2.4	(3.8 km)	96
(52)	Springhill Ponds	4.4	(7.0 km)	97
(53)	Springhill Ponds from the South	3.0	(4.8 km)	99
(54)	Whortleberry Pond	0.3	(0.5 km)	100
(55)	Sucker Brook and Desolate Brook Trail to Pharaoh Lake	7.5	(12.1 km)	101
(56)	Spectacle Pond	1.7	(2.9 km)	102
(57)	Gull Pond	0.5	(0.8 km)	103
(58)	Severance Mt.	1.2	(2.0 km)	103
(59)	Cook Mt.	1.7	(2.7 km)	104
(60)	Rogers Rock	1.1	(1.8 km)	106

(36) Crane Pond Rd.

Trails Illustrated Map #743: S28

The Crane Pond Rd. is one of the major northern access points for the Pharaoh Lake Wilderness. Within a reasonable distance from the parking lot are trails to Pharaoh Mt., Pharaoh Lake, and many of the interior ponds. At present (October 2004) this road is considered closed to motorized vehicles by DEC, but access is not blocked.

▶ Trailhead: From the intersection of US 9 and NY 74 at I-87 Exit 28, just N of Schroon Lake, head S on US 9. Take the first L (E) on Alder Meadow Rd. (indicated by the sign for the airport). Go 2.2 mi to a L (E) fork in the road and continue another 2.4 mi on a narrow road to the Crane Pond parking lot. The road beyond this point is in classified Wilderness and most likely will at some time be blocked to vehicular traffic. The section of the road from the parking lot to Crane Pond isn't plowed in the winter. ◀

FROM THE PARKING LOT (0.0 mi), the road to Crane Pond changes minimally in elevation. At 0.9 mi is the trailhead for the Goose Pond trail (37) on the R (S). Some sections of the road from here to Crane

Pond are quite rough, with "Wilson Hill" claiming numerous mufflers each year. At 1.6 mi, the NE end of Alder Pond may be flooded. A yellow-marked foot trail heads L just before the hairpin turn before the flooded area of road. At approx. 1.7 mi the Long Swing Trail (trail 38) from NY 74 comes in from the L. The W end of Crane Pond is reached at 2.0 mi.

※ Distances: Parking lot to Goose Pond (trail 37), 0.9 mi; to Long Swing Trail, 1.7 mi; to Crane Pond, 2.0 mi (3.0 km).

(37) **Goose Pond**

Trails Illustrated Map #743: S28

▶ Trailhead: The Goose Pond trailhead is on the S side of Crane Pond Rd. 0.9 mi from the Crane Pond parking lot at the wilderness edge (see trail 36 trailhead description). ◀

THE TRAIL LEAVES from the S side of the road (0.0 mi) and has yellow trail markers. Goose Pond is special trout water. (See regulations in the introduction to this section.)

At 0.1 mi, the trail crosses a high plank bridge over the outlet of Alder Pond. Upstream a beaver dam can be seen. At 0.2 mi, the trail crosses a mossy log bridge over a wet place and soon another mossy log bridge. Now the trail goes gently uphill over rocks and roots, leveling off at 0.3 mi, then rising again. This section is heavily used and eroded down to mud and tree roots in places.

The trail goes gently downhill and at 0.5 mi Goose Pond can be seen glistening through the hemlocks. At 0.6 mi, the trail reaches a campsite near the edge of the pond. Across the pond is a view of Pharaoh Mt. A trail to the L skirts a bay and loops back to the main trail. Mergansers and loons may be seen here.

※ Distance: Trailhead to Goose Pond, 0.6 mi (1.0 km).

(38) **Long Swing Trail to Crane Pond Rd.**

Trails Illustrated Map #743: S28

▶ Trailhead: From Northway (I-87) Exit 28, cross US 9 heading E on NY 74. Go 4.2 mi to a small parking area on the R with the DEC sign for Crane Pond. The trailhead is only 0.1 mi W of the Paradox Lake State Campground entrance. ◀

THE TRAIL CLIMBS up the bank from the parking area (0.0 mi) and enters woods. It goes back (W) parallel to the road, crosses a cedar log bridge over a stream, and soon turns L (S) onto an older trail, marked with blue trail markers. The woods are mature white pine, hemlock, sugar maple, and yellow birch.

At 0.2 mi, a smaller hemlock grows so close to a giant white pine that they look like Mutt and Jeff. The trail now heads S away from the road and is quite level. At 0.3 mi, the trail crosses a bridge over the stream, under tall trees that include some enormous yellow birch.

Now the trail heads uphill along the stream and under tall hemlocks. At 0.4 mi, it crosses the stream on rocks. The trail heads uphill, then levels off again at 0.5 mi and skirts a beaver flow on the R side of the flooded marked trail for a short distance.

At 0.7 mi, a new beaver pond filled with dead trees opens up the sky. The trail crosses a bridge over the outlet, with Blue Hill in view ahead. It follows the edge of the pond, then gently ascends at 0.9 mi. At 1.0 mi, the trail starts to descend; at 1.1 mi, it heads down more steeply. At 1.2 mi, it levels out at two hemlocks with old gashes, possibly the original trailmarkers.

At 1.7 mi, the trail crosses a stream on rocks, then climbs the bank and levels again. It continues to climb until it levels at 1.9 mi. After passing some giant maples at 2.0 mi, the trail continues uphill through dense hemlock, beech, and birch. At 2.3 mi, near its northern limit, there is an enormous red oak.

Now the trail goes gently downhill. At 2.8 mi is a T intersection with the narrow dirt road to Crane Pond (trail 36). Turn L to walk another 0.3 mi to Crane Pond and the trailhead to Pharaoh Mt.

⚹ Distances: NY 74 to beaver pond, 0.7 mi; to Crane Pond Rd. (trail 36), 2.8 mi (4.5 km). To Crane Pond, 3.1 mi (5.1 km).

(39) Tubmill Marsh Trail
(39A) Crab Pond Spur to Glidden Marsh Trail

Trails Illustrated Map #743: S29

This trail from the N leads in to the Pharaoh Lake Wilderness and connects to the trails leading to the many ponds in the northern Pharaoh region. It also connects directly with some of the interior trails for easy access to Pharaoh Lake and Pharaoh Mt. for nice hiking and backpacking loops through the region.

▶ Trailhead: A large trailhead sign on the R (S) side of NY 74 8.1 mi E of Exit 28 on I-87 (the Adirondack Northway) marks the start. The trail has blue markers; the spur from Crab Pond to Glidden Marsh (trail 39A) is marked in red. ◀

FROM THE PARKING LOT (0.0 mi), the trail heads E, parallel to the road, above a wetland with beaver activity, then uphill through woods of cedar, oak, birch, hemlock, and white pine, reaching the Eagle Lake dam at 0.3 mi. After crossing a bridge, the trail turns R (W) and follows the S side of the outlet stream. The fairly level trail soon crosses concrete culverts at 0.6 mi and then heads gradually uphill at 0.8 mi. After leveling off for a bit, the trail begins a long gradual decline until it reaches an intersection at 1.0 mi with two private trails from the Pyramid Lake Camp.

Bearing L (SW) around the base of Ragged Mt., the trail soon begins ascending through the pass between Ragged Mt. on the L (E), and Bear Mt. on the R (W). At 1.8 mi, it reaches the top of a triple col between Ragged Mt., Bear Mt., and Potter Mt. at about 1300 ft. After a descent along a side hill, the side trail for the Tubmill Marsh lean-to departs R (W) at 2.2 mi. The lean-to is 0.1 mi on this spur, and it's about 500 ft downhill to the marsh from the lean-to. This is a great place to see wildlife and is pretty when the blue flags are blooming in summer.

A sign indicating the way to Honey Pond is at 2.4 mi. After crossing a couple of streams, the trail cuts up along a ridge to a beaver pond at 2.9 mi. Across the beaver pond is a view of Big Clear Pond Mt., elev. 2000 ft, about 500 ft above the beaver pond.

The trail soon crosses a stream and turns away from the pond.

At 3.2 mi, the trail turns R and goes around Honey Pond and along a high ridge into a stand of birches. At 3.4 mi, it reaches the jct. with the trail to Lilypad Pond (trail 45) coming in from the L (E). It is 1.8 mi along this trail to Rock Pond; the Lilypad Pond Lean-to is very near the intersection.

Continuing S, the trail climbs for a short distance and then passes an old indistinct side trail for Treadway Mt. at 3.8 mi. The trail soon crosses the outlet of a small pond, and at 4.2 mi Horseshoe Pond comes into view. Soon there is an angler's trail to the R, across an old beaver dam. The trail descends along the outlet of the pond and then crosses the inlet to Crab Pond, which is soon visible through the hemlocks.

The trail crosses another inlet stream and continues along the S side of the pond, reaching a jct. at 4.9 mi. L is the Crab Pond Spur Trail (trail 39A), a direct route 0.4 mi S from Crab Pond to the Glidden Marsh Trail (41). It is marked with red markers.

Continuing straight (W) around the outlet of Crab Pond, the trail reaches Oxshoe Pond at 5.4 mi and the Oxshoe Pond Lean-to at 5.6 mi. It's a pretty view from the lean-to with rock ledges and pines around the shore of the pond.

At 5.9 mi, the trail reaches the shoreline of Glidden Marsh and intersects with the W end of the Glidden Marsh Trail (trail 41). Turning R, the trail heads NW, away from the shoreline, and enters a nice hemlock forest. After crossing a bridge, the trail climbs slightly and intersects the Pharaoh Mt. Trail (trail 40) at 6.4 mi. From here it is 0.7 mi to the end of the road at Crane Pond (trail 36).

𑁍 Distances: Parking lot at NY 74 to Tubmill Marsh lean-to cutoff, 2.2 mi; to Rock Pond/Lilypad Pond Trail (trail 45), 3.4 mi; to Crab Pond jct., 4.9 mi; to Oxshoe Pond lean-to, 5.6 mi; to Glidden Marsh Trail (trail 41), 5.9 mi; to Pharaoh Mt. Trail (trail 40), 6.4 mi (10.2 km). Distance of Crab Pond Spur Trail (trail 39A), 0.4 mi (0.6 km).

(40) Pharaoh Mt. Trail (Crane Pond to Pharaoh Lake)
(40A) Lean-to Spur Trail

Trails Illustrated Map #743: R–S28

Pharaoh Mt. is a very dominant feature when looking across Schroon Lake from the Northway into the Pharaoh region. It rises sharply from the landscape with its steep rock faces dominating the W side. It's a pleasant mountain to climb, and the views offer an all-round perspective on the eastern Adirondack region.

▶ Trailhead: The red-marked trail starts at the W end of Crane Pond, at the end of Crane Pond Rd. (trail 36). ◀

LEAVING CRANE POND RD. (0.0 mi), the trail crosses a plank bridge at the outlet of Crane Pond. A trail register is a short distance along the trail past the bridge. It follows an old tote road through a pretty woods of tall evergreens. At 0.7 mi, the trail reaches a jct. with the Glidden Marsh trail to Pharaoh Lake (trail 41). The trail to Pharaoh Mt. bears R by an old cellar hole. It soon passes a beaver pond, Glidden Marsh on the L, and big white pines.

The trail begins ascending at 1.9 mi, soon bearing R and becoming steeper. At 2.0 mi, it crosses a stream (dry in late summer). Now the trail is fairly steep and eroded down to rock. At 2.8 mi, at a good view, the trail is on an open ridge of bare rock. The top isn't far away.

The trail soon reaches the site where the observer's cabin once stood and then at 2.9 mi the open rock summit where the fire tower once stood. The actual summit is just a short distance to the N of the observer's cabin site.

There are great views to the High Peaks and Hoffman Notch Wilderness across Schroon Lake from the rock ledges on the W side of the summit. By exploring the summit to the N and E it is possible to view the High Peaks, the NE Adirondacks, Lake Champlain and Vermont, Pharaoh Lake, and the mountains of the Pharaoh Lake Wilderness. Try to pick out Crane Mt. to the SW and the Tongue Mt. Range to the SE.

The route continuing across the summit and down the E side of the mountain is a pleasant, lightly used trail. From the site of the old observer's cabin, the trail heads E across the summit. After a couple of short, steep descents, at 3.2 mi (mileage from Crane Pond) the route crosses a stream, soon comes to an opening, then crosses the stream again. At 3.5 mi there is an outlook to the rocky face of Treadway Mt. to the NE. There are blueberries here, in season, along the open rock, as well as trailing arbutus which is on the NYS list of protected plants. At 3.7 mi, the clearing ends and soon Pharaoh Lake can be seen below. After crossing and then recrossing a stream, the trail goes over a couple of bridges and wooden walkways, coming close to the shoreline of Pharaoh Lake at 4.5 mi.

Turning R (S) along the shore of the lake, the trail parallels the shoreline, passing over a couple of streams, then a wetland on the L, and reaches a jct. with a side trail at 5.3 mi. This Lean-to Spur Trail (trail 40A) leads to Pharaoh lean-to #5 and the point that protrudes into the lake. There are great views from the tip of the point, 0.2 mi from the main trail.

Continuing along the main trail, there is another lean-to (#6) visible through the trees at 5.7 mi. The outlet of the lake and the jct. with the Mill Brook Trail (trail 50) are at 6.2 mi. It is 2.5 mi to the parking lot at Mill Brook and 3.6 mi to the parking lot by the wilderness boundary via trail 50.

❋ Trail in winter: This is an excellent ski-shoeing route in the winter, skiing in on the road and part way up the trail, then snowshoeing to the summit. A group could return the same way, or continue down the other side, skiing out the Pharaoh/Mill Brook Trail (trail 50) to another car parked at the end of the access road.

⅍ Distances: Crane Pond Rd. (trail 36) to Glidden Marsh Trail (trail 41), 0.7 mi; to summit, 2.9 mi; to shore of Pharaoh Lake, 4.5 mi; to side trail to lean-tos, 5.3 mi; to Pharaoh Lake via Mill Brook trail (trail 50), 6.2 mi (9.9 km). Ascent from Crane Pond, 1470 ft (448 m); ascent from Pharaoh Lake, 1390 ft (424 m). Elevation of Pharaoh Mt., 2551 ft (778 m).

(41) Glidden Marsh to Pharaoh Lake

Trails Illustrated Map #743: R28–29

This trail connects the Crane Pond area with the Pharaoh Lake area and the Grizzle Ocean Trail (trail 47). This way it's possible to hike from the Crane Pond area to the Pharaoh Lake area, then up to the Putnam Pond area (trail 43), and back to Crane Pond via Crab Pond and Oxshoe Pond (trails 45 and 39) without having to retrace many of your steps. It's a long route, but it would make a nice two- to four-day backpacking trip (depending on how much time you have to relax and enjoy or explore).

▶ Trailhead: The yellow-marked Glidden Marsh Trail begins along Glidden Marsh at a jct. with the Tubmill Marsh Trail (trail 39), 0.4 mi E of the Pharaoh Mt. Trail (trail 40), and 1.1 mi from the end of Crane Pond Rd. (trail 36). ◀

GLIDDEN MARSH is a great place to see wildlife. Herons and other waterfowl frequent this area and there is a lot of beaver sign.

At the jct. with the Tubmill Marsh Trail (trail 39) (0.0 mi), the trail heads SE along the shore of Glidden Marsh. The trail soon begins a gradual ascent and at 0.6 mi reaches a jct. on the L with the Crab Pond Spur Trail (trail 39A). There is a sign here for Crab Pond 0.4 mi to the L.

The trail now climbs very gradually through the rolling woods on the E side of Pharaoh Mt., crosses a couple of streams, and passes a small pond. At 2.1 mi, it begins a fairly steep descent toward Pharaoh Lake, coming near the shoreline at 3.1 mi, where a sign indicates a turn L. The trail now follows to the E around Split Rock Bay on Pharaoh Lake, and then swings S along the bay toward a lean-to. At 3.7 mi, the trail reaches

Pharo Lean-to (#4) on a fine broad point with views of the lake.

Heading E, the trail soon crosses a stream and then heads more S and away from the lake. Passing a side trail for Wintergreen Point (0.3 mi, with some great views), the trail almost immediately comes to a jct. with the Grizzle Ocean Trail (trail 47) and the East Shore of Pharaoh Lake Trail (trail 51) at 4.4 mi.

⚕ Distances: Tubmill Marsh Trail (trail 39) to Crab Pond Spur Trail, 0.6 mi; to Pharaoh Lake, 3.1 mi; to Pharo Lean-to, 3.7 mi; to Grizzle Ocean Trail (trail 47) and East Shore of Pharaoh Lake Trail (trail 51), 4.4 mi (7.0 km).

(42) Otter Pond

Trails Illustrated Map #743: S29

This is the only pond in this area that is open for public access. There have been serious trespassing problems here. The only legal public access is from the boat launch on Eagle Lake, since the shoreline on the S side of the road is privately owned. You may not drive your vehicle on the private road. There is no public access to Gooseneck Pond on this road. Be sure to follow the trail directions with absolute care.

▶ Trailhead: On NY 74, approximately 9.5 mi E of I-87 (Adirondack Northway) Exit 28 (approx. 8.0 mi W of Ticonderoga), is a boat access site for Eagle Lake, just W of the causeway. It is a short canoe trip almost due S across the lake to the trailhead and sign for Otter Pond in a small cove on the SE shore of Eagle Lake. ◀

FROM THE CANOE LANDING (0.0 mi), walk L on the road along the shore for 0.1 mi to a low place on the R where two dark blue DEC trail markers lead into the woods. The trail is well marked, but the start is easy to miss.

Continuing on the level for a short time, the trail quickly goes uphill. It climbs steeply through a draw on an N-facing slope of hemlocks and boulders. The trail is so little used that you must depend on the trail markers. At 0.2 mi, the trail levels, curves L, and goes gently uphill to Otter Pond at 0.3 mi. Trail markers on the trees here show that the beavers are busy at work. To the R at about 100 ft is a beaver dam at the outlet.

⚕ Distance: Canoe landing to Otter Pond, 0.3 mi (0.5 km).

(43)   **Clear Pond Trail**
(43A) **Rock Pond Spur**
(43B) **West Clear Pond Trail**
(43C) **Putnam Pond to Clear Pond Trail**

Trails Illustrated Map #743: R–S29

This trail circles around the Putnam Pond area and provides access to the several small ponds W of Putnam Pond. When the Clear Pond trail is combined with a portion of the Grizzle Ocean Trail (trail 47), it's possible to make a complete circuit of Putnam Pond.

▶ Trailhead: Drive 13.3 mi E on NY 74 from I-87 (Adirondack Northway) Exit 28 (Ticonderoga–Paradox) to a large sign on the R for Putnam Pond State Campground. Drive S 3.8 mi to the entrance. Day-use fees are charged in season. A boat launch is just beyond on the R and the parking lot is at 4.2 mi (0.4 mi from the entrance). From the parking lot, walk along the entrance road 0.4 mi to the entrance booth, then another 0.4 mi in to the campground to the trailhead at campsites 38 and 39. The trail is marked with yellow markers to the end of Clear Pond, and then blue markers from Clear Pond to its jct. with the Grizzle Ocean Trail (trail 47). ◀

STARTING AT CAMPSITES **38** AND **39** (0.0 mi), the trail heads N toward Heart Pond. It crosses and recrosses a stream, reaching the jct. with Bear Pond Trail (trail 44) at 0.4 mi. Continuing L to the S of Heart Pond, at 0.5 mi the trail passes a spur to the N that goes to a point that overlooks this pretty little pond.

The trail continues W over rolling terrain, follows the N shoreline of North Pond, and crosses a bridge at 1.1 mi. At 1.5 mi, the trail reaches the shore of North Pond. (North Pond is actually a long extended bay to the N of Putnam Pond.) The trail heads W, climbs up and then descends over a hill, and reaches a jct. with the Rock Pond Spur trail (trail 43A) at 1.7 mi.

Turn L (S) at this jct. for the main trail and the shortest route to Clear Pond, as well as the Little Rock Pond Lean-to. The trail crosses a stream and comes to the lean-to at 1.9 mi, meeting up with the Rock Pond Spur Trail again at 2.0 mi.

[The Rock Pond Spur trail (43A) heads straight (W) at the jct. at 1.7 mi to a jct. with the Rock Pond to Lilypad Pond Trail (45) at Rock Pond in 0.2 mi. Turn L (S) at the trail 45 intersection to follow S along the E shore of Rock Pond, passing the Rock Pond Lean-to at 0.4 mi and meeting up with the Clear Pond Trail at 0.5 mi. This spur is 0.5 mi long, or 0.1 mi longer than the parallel section of the main trail.]

From the jct. at 2.0 mi, trail 43 continues S, with Rock Pond to the W and Little Rock Pond to the E. It crosses an isthmus that separates the two ponds, and then comes to another jct. at 2.1 mi. The trail to the R (W) is the S route of the Rock Pond to Lilypad Pond Trail (trail 45).

Trail 43 continues on to the S, ascending and then descending to the trail jct. at the head of Clear Pond at 2.7 mi. Here again there's a choice, to go around the E or the W side of Clear Pond. The West Clear Pond Trail (trail 43B) is the shorter by about 0.1 mi at 0.6 mi. It heads R at this intersection, following the W side of Clear Pond and rejoining the main trail.

The main trail heads L around the E shoreline of Clear Pond, reaching the Clear Pond lean-to at 3.1 mi. Behind the lean-to is the Putnam Pond to Clear Pond Trail (trail 43C), running 0.6 mi to Putnam Pond. Continuing on the main trail at the outlet of Clear Pond, the jct. with the trail along the W side of the pond is at 3.4 mi.

Trail 43 continues S and E past Mud Pond to an intersection with the Treadway Mt. Trail (trail 46) at 3.6 mi. Continuing S across the intersection, the trail soon meets the Grizzle Ocean Trail (trail 47) at 4.0 mi. The trail L (E) leads to the Putnam Pond parking lot in 1.4 mi.

⚹ Distances: Putnam Pond campsites 38 and 39 to Bear Pond Trail (trail 44), 0.4 mi; to trail to Little Rock Pond and Rock Pond, 1.7 mi; to Little Rock Pond Lean-to, 1.9 mi; to Rock Pond Lean-to, 2.1 mi; to Clear Pond lean-to and side trail to Putnam Pond, 3.1 mi; to Treadway Mt. Trail (trail 46), 3.6 mi; to Grizzle Ocean Trail (trail 47), 4.0 mi (6.4 km). Length of trail 43A spur, 0.5 mi (0.8 km); length of trail 43B, 0.6

mi (1.0 km); length of trail 43C spur, 0.6 mi (1.0 km). Complete circuit of Putnam Pond with return via Grizzle Ocean Trail (trail 47) to parking lot, 6.2 mi (9.9 km).

(44) Bear Pond Trail

Trails Illustrated Map #743: S29

This is a trail to one of the special trout waters in the Pharaoh Lake Wilderness area. (See the regulations in this section's introduction.) The trail connects with the Clear Pond Trail (trail 43) at Heart Pond at the E end and the North Rock Pond Trail (trail 45A) on the W end. There is no public access other than the Clear Pond Trail.

▶ Trailhead: The easiest access to this trail is via the Clear Pond Trail from Putnam Pond campsites 38 and 39 (see trail 43). It is 0.4 mi N on the Clear Pond Trail from the campsites to the beginning of the Bear Pond Trail. The trail is marked with blue markers. ◀

LEAVING THE HEART POND JCT. with the Clear Pond Trail (trail 43) (0.0 mi), the trail heads N along the E shore of Heart Pond. At 1.0 mi, it crosses open rocky places with blueberry bushes before descending a small hill to a L (S) turn near Bear Pond at 1.2 mi. Here an unmaintained trail leads to private land.

The trail soon leads over a small knoll to a campsite on the E shore of Bear Pond. There are lots of signs of beaver activity around the pond. Heading S, the trail soon reaches the edge of Bear Pond and then follows along a narrow, rocky path. The trail passes along the marshy SE corner of the pond with rocky cliffs on the L, crosses an inlet stream, and soon leaves the pond at 1.5 mi.

The trail gradually heads uphill, up and over Bear Pond Mt., reaching height of land at 2.2 mi, elev. approx. 1750 ft, 350 ft above Bear Pond. The trail is rather washed out for a while, then levels off on a hemlock-studded hillside before descending gradually along some rock cliffs. At 2.7 mi, it drops more steeply to Rock Pond, now visible through the trees. At 2.8 mi, the trail reaches the Rock Pond to Lilypad Pond trail (45). L is the Rock Pond Spur trail (43A) in 0.2 mi. Across the pond are Peaked Hill and Little Clear Pond.

🡒 Distances: Heart Pond jct. on Clear Pond Trail to Bear Pond, 1.2 mi; to height of land, 2.2 mi; to Rock Pond to Lilypad Pond Trail, 2.8 mi (4.5 km).

(45) Rock Pond to Lilypad Pond
(45A) North Rock Pond Trail

Trails Illustrated Map #743: S29

This trail, besides being the connector trail between the Putnam Pond area on the E and the Crab Pond and Crane Pond area on the W, is a pleasant trail to hike. There are fine views from the shoreline of Rock Pond, and it's a nice walk along Rock Pond Brook to Lilypad Pond Lean-to. It's also possible to make a loop around Rock Pond using part of the Clear Pond Trail (trail 43).

▶ Trailhead: From its E end, this red-marked trail begins at the SE corner of Rock Pond, near Little Rock Pond at a jct. with the Clear Pond Trail (trail 43). ◀

FROM THE CLEAR POND TRAIL (trail 43) near Little Rock Pond (0.0 mi), the trail heads W around the S shore of Rock Pond. It soon follows the shoreline and heads N along the W shore, passing a campsite on a nice promontory on the W side of the pond. At 0.7 mi it meets trail 45A (see below) on the S side of Rock Pond outlet.

Heading W from the jct., trail 45 parallels the outlet stream for some distance. At 1.2 mi, a waterfall is heard off to the R. In a short distance the trail descends to the waterfall, where there is a short side trail leading to the falls. The trail now begins following along a wetland until at 1.8 mi it climbs and reaches Lilypad Pond Lean-to at Lilypad Pond. From the lean-to it's a short distance to the jct. with the Tubmill Marsh Trail (trail 39) at 1.9 mi.

TRAIL 45A STARTS from the NE corner of Rock Pond, on the Rock Pond Spur trail (43A) at a point 1.9 mi from the Putnam Pond State Campground. It heads W along the alluring N side of Rock Pond. At 0.2 mi, the Bear Pond Trail (trail 44) intersects on the R. Shortly after a turn R, there is a cave-like entrance to an old graphite mine with some brownish water seeping from it.

The trail climbs steeply uphill to a bluff on the L that overlooks the pond. A side trail leads to a rock point with some blueberry bushes and several large white pines on the end.

The trail soon passes a campsite with a fireplace, then follows the shoreline, climbs steeply to some more open rock at 0.4 mi, and drops steeply once again to the shoreline. At 0.7 mi there is another campsite on a huge open rock. It may be easy to lose the trail here because of the rock. Continue straight through the clearing to the trail, which crosses the outlet of Rock Pond to trail 45 at 0.8 mi.

⚔ Distances: Clear Pond Trail (trail 43) to jct. with trail 45A at Rock Pond outlet, 0.7 mi; Lilypad Pond lean-to, 1.8 mi; to Tubmill Marsh Trail (trail 39), 1.9 mi (3.0 km). Length of trail 45A, 0.8 mi (1.3 km).

(46) Treadway Mt. Trail

Trails Illustrated Map #743: R29

This is a unique mountain with large open rocky spaces on top and an interior trail that winds along a U-shaped summit. Trailing arbutus and blueberries grow profusely along the upper parts of the trail. There are good views of Treadway's more popular neighbor, Pharaoh Mt., and surrounding points, as well as the High Peaks and more mountains to the W, S, and E. It is possible to cross Putnam Pond by canoe to the Treadway Mt. trailhead, which removes 3.6 mi from a round trip.

Pharaoh Lake from Treadway Mt. JEFFREY TRUBISZ

▶ Trailhead: The trailhead is 1.4 mi S on the Grizzle Ocean Trail (trail 47) from Putnam Pond State Campground, then 0.4 mi N on the Clear Pond Trail (trail 43). At a jct. at this point, the Treadway Mt. Trail goes L; R leads 0.2 mi to the landing for the canoe short-cut. To reach the Treadway Mt. trailhead on Putnam Pond by canoe, put in at the boat launch on the E shore near the Putnam Pond parking lot (see trail 43). Then canoe W and S to a small point on the W shore of Putnam Pond. The trail starts by a small stream in the cove behind the point. The trail is marked with red markers. ◀

FROM THE CLEAR POND TRAIL (trail 43) (0.0 mi), the red-marked trail proceeds 0.1 mi to a deadwood swamp called Mud Pond. Wintergreen grows along the edge of the trail, which follows the S side of Mud Pond. At 0.2 mi, the trail crosses a stream on a log with a beaver dam downstream, turning L along the stream. At 0.3 mi, it crosses the stream and soon recrosses it. Now it climbs moderately and can be wet. It is a wide old tote road through hemlocks, with a stream on the R, and then mixed hardwoods.

At 0.9 mi, the trail comes to a swamp with bright green grass and moss. It becomes steeper at 1.1 mi above a swampy stream. At 1.2 mi, it becomes rocky, winding above a ravine to the L. Then it arrives at the first bare rock with trailing arbutus and a cairn at 1.3 mi. It is important to follow the red paint blazes on the rock. In early July, bright pink sheep laurel blooms here.

At 1.5 mi, the trail climbs through a chimney and arrives in a thick growth of blueberry bushes. At 1.6 mi, it goes into woods again; at 1.7 mi is the first view to the E. At 1.8 mi, the trail comes to the bottom of a dip. Then at 2.0 mi it reaches a false summit and after another dip arrives at the true summit at 2.1 mi.

This mountain deserves more attention; it has a varied and satisfying climb and fascinating summit trail over its open rocky top. Views are excellent.

❊ Trail in winter: This would make an excellent snowshoe trip and enjoyable, advanced-level ski trip. Some distance could be saved by cutting straight across Putnam Pond to the trail, as can be done in summer with a canoe.

⚼ Distances: Clear Pond Trail to cairn, 1.3 mi; to chimney, 1.5 mi; to summit, 2.1 mi (3.5 km). Parking lot to summit, 3.9 mi (6.5 km). Ascent, approx. 900 ft (275 m). Summit elevation, 2240 ft (683 m).

By canoe: paddle approx. 1.0 mi across Putnam Pond from boat launch
SW to a small point. Walk on trail with red markers 0.2 mi to a jct.,
then straight to summit at approx. 2.3 mi (3.8 km).

(47) Grizzle Ocean Trail
(47A) Grizzle Ocean Circuit Trail

Trails Illustrated Map #743: R29

This fairly easy trail connects the Putnam Pond and Pharaoh Lake areas.
▶ Trailhead: The trail begins on the W side of the parking lot at
Putnam Pond State Campground. (For directions to the parking lot, see
the Clear Pond Trail [trail 43].) The trail has yellow markers. ◀

THE TRAIL IMMEDIATELY CROSSES a pair of bridges. A side trail goes
R to Putnam Pond. At 0.3 mi the trail crosses a muddy place, and then
crosses a brook. At 0.7 mi, the trail goes downhill through hemlocks
with a mossy cliff on the L and soon crosses an inlet to the pond on a
plank bridge. At 1.2 mi, it reaches a jct. (An unmarked side trail R goes
to the S edge of Putnam Pond.) The trail crosses a brook on a plank
bridge. At 1.4 mi it reaches a stream with a bridge. On the other side
a trail R leads via Clear Pond Trail (trail 43) back to Putnam Pond State
Campground, circling Putnam Pond.

The main trail heads L (S) to Grizzle Ocean. At 1.6 mi it crosses the
stream on rocks, and at 1.8 mi reaches a height of land. (The Grizzle
Ocean Lean-to spur goes L 0.2 mi, following blue trail markers. The
lean-to is set back under pines from the edge of Grizzle Ocean, a pretty, shallow pond in spite of its name.)

From the lean-to spur, the trail continues to a long wooden walkway
which crosses the outlet of Grizzle Ocean at 2.0 mi. The trail turns L
at the end of the walkway and at 2.1 mi reaches a jct. with the red-
marked Grizzle Ocean Circuit Trail (trail 47A) around

Grizzle Ocean is on the L. [This trail circles the pond and reaches the
lean-to in 0.9 mi. It is 0.2 mi from the lean-to following yellow markers back to the Grizzle Ocean Trail for a total of 1.1 mi (1.8 km) around
the E side of Grizzle Ocean. Turn R to continue to Pharaoh Lake.]

At 2.2 mi, the trail reaches a miniature pond on the R. At 2.5 mi, it
crosses a small stream on rocks and soon crosses the stream again. At
2.8 mi, it reaches a wet place which is the start of a stream under high
maples, and begins to follow the stream downhill. This is the divide

between Putnam Pond and Pharaoh Lake. It is also a pass between Grizzle Ocean Mt. to the N and Thunderbolt Mt. to the S.

At 3.3 mi, the trail comes to a very muddy spot, then a couple of streams. It goes along a hillside with hemlocks and maples at 3.7 mi, then crosses a bridge. At 3.8 mi, it reaches a small stream tumbling down through rocks, from Devil's Washdish. At 3.9 mi, the trail passes Wolf Pond on the L, seen through the trees, It reaches an inlet to Wolf Pond at 4.0 mi, and another at 4.1 mi.

Now the trail goes along a fern-filled hillside above a swampy area. It follows a ridge, and then passes through a grove of hemlocks. It descends and at 4.4 mi travels over some rolling terrain.

At 4.6 mi, the trail reaches the top of another small hill and at 4.8 mi it reaches an algae-filled bay. At 5.1 mi, it crosses a stream that feeds into Pharaoh Lake and then passes under a tall stand of red pines; a waterfall is audible down to the L.

At 5.2 mi, the trail reaches an intersection at Pharaoh Lake. The Glidden Marsh trail (41) R goes to Wintergreen Point and to Pharaoh Lean-to at Split Rock Bay. The East Shore of Pharaoh Lake trail (trail 51) L goes along the E shore of Pharaoh Lake. Just before this trail jct. it is about 100 ft downhill through the woods to a view of the waterfall. From the jct. it is 0.1 mi L to a good plank bridge directly below the waterfall. This is a good place for a rest stop and picnic, with a good view of Wintergreen Point and its shallow bay filled with pond lilies.

⋈ Distances: Putnam Pond State Campground parking lot to Clear Pond Trail (trail 43), 1.4 mi; to Grizzle Ocean Lean-to jct, 1.8 mi; to watershed divide, 2.8 mi; to Pharaoh Lake, 5.2 mi (8.3 km); to waterfall and plank bridge, 5.3 mi (9.1 km).

(48) **Berrymill Flow from the North**

Trails Illustrated Map #743: R29

▶ Trailhead: The trailhead is near the exit of the parking area in the Putnam Pond State Campground (see trail 43). Maps, including the one used as the base map for this book, identify the flow as Berrymill Pond, but trail signs, and consequently this book, refer to it as Berrymill Flow. ◀

THE TRAIL STARTS UPHILL on an old tote road, crosses a stream, and soon enters a straight section, following blue markers. At 0.4 mi, the road goes up along the brook on the R. At 0.6 mi, it crosses a stream and then travels at a gentle pace through the woods. At 1.5 mi, the trail crosses a clearing and another stream where there may be some beaver activity. The marked side trail R (W) to the pond and the lean-to is at 2.0 mi, near the outlet of this sinuous body of water.

✳ Trail in winter: This is ideal as a gentle ski or snowshoe trip.

🐾 Distance: Parking lot to pond and lean-to, 2.0 mi (3.2 km).

(48A) Berrymill Flow from the South

Trails Illustrated Map #743: Q–R30

▶ Trailhead: This trailhead is reached from the town of Hague. Turn R (N) onto Summit Drive from NY 8, 3.0 mi W of Hague (0.0 mi). At 0.8 mi, take the sharp R curve. The road soon joins with West Hague Rd. and at 1.4 mi passes May Memorial Cemetery on the R (E). At 2.0 mi there is a small trailhead parking lot and sign for Berrymill Flow on the L (W) side of the road. The trail follows yellow markers for 0.3 mi and then forks R with blue markers. Maps, including the one used as the base map for this book, identify the flow as Berrymill Pond, but trail signs, and consequently this book, refer to it as Berrymill Flow. ◀

FROM THE PARKING LOT (0.0 mi), the trail starts uphill and at 0.3 mi there is a jct. with the Springhill Ponds from the South trail (trail 53) on the L. Bear R and continue the gradual climb. The trail becomes steeper at 1.2 mi, and then levels off at 1.3 mi. It passes a wetland at 1.5 mi, then crosses a couple of bridges and a stream and beaver flow with uprooted trees at 2.2 mi. A spring is passed at 2.6 mi, just before a bridge. The jct. on the L for Berrymill Flow is at 3.0 mi, with the shore of the pond at 3.1 mi. Turning R, there is an old lean-to site at 3.2 mi. After a knoll of white and red pine, the trail reaches the end of this point at 3.4 mi. Blueberries grow in abundance here, as do trailing arbutus and ladyslippers. There are signs of beaver activity in the cove to the R, where there is also a lean-to.

To reach the lean-to, go back to the jct. at 3.0 mi. Head L (N) about 100 yd to another jct. with a sign for Putnam Pond 1.9 mi to the R and Berrymill lean-to to the L. Another 100 yd to the L (W) is the lean-to on the cove.

✳ Trail in winter: Suitable for snowshoeing.

♔ Distances: W. Hague Rd. parking to wetland, 1.5 mi; to first Berrymill Flow jct., 3.0 mi; to lean-to, 3.2 mi (5.1 km).

(49) **Lost Pond**

Trails Illustrated Map #743: R29–30

▶ Trailhead: From NY 74 at Chilson, turn S onto the road with a large sign for Putnam Pond State Campground and drive 3.3 mi to the trailhead sign for Lost Pond on the L. The trail is an old tote road with yellow markers. This is a well-used trail popular with campers and anglers. The pond's outlet is underground for a quarter mile adjacent to the trail. ◀

DEPARTING FROM THE TRAILHEAD SIGN (0.0 mi), at 0.3 mi the old road enters a stand of hemlocks. There are lots of Indian pipes growing here in July. At 0.4 mi, the trail forks L from the old road. There are exposed roots of beech and maple trees. At 0.5 mi, the trail goes over a knoll, into a dip, and then up another knoll. Here it levels off. At 0.7 mi, it navigates a muddy seep.

At 0.9 mi, the trail descends gently before going through woods of maple, beech, and huge birches. At 1.0 mi, it reaches a plank bridge over a stream with huge boulders. A beaver swamp is down to the L. White orchids may be seen growing here on the R in July. The trail passes the outlet of the pond at 1.1 mi, then a private trail on the L over a stream. At 1.2 mi, the trail crosses the stream, continuing uphill. At 1.3 mi, the trail levels out among mature maples. At 1.4 mi, Lost Pond is in sight, and soon the trail reaches a jct. for a trail around the pond.

Continuing R around the pond, yellow markers are very helpful since the path is sometimes faint. There has been a fair amount of beaver activity at this pond. At 1.7 mi, the trail comes along a mossy cliff on the R, then crosses a rocky stream at 1.8 mi. At 1.9 mi, the trail comes around one of the end lobes of the pond. At 2.0 mi, it reaches an outcropping of boulders. This is a good picnic spot. Trout fishing is quite good. Chickadees, warblers, thrushes, and veeries sing their various songs along the edge of the deep forest.

In a few hundred yards there is a campsite with a fire circle. Another campsite is at 2.2 mi. Blueberries are thick along the trail here in summer.

Now the trail climbs steeply up through boulders along Abe's Hill. At 2.5 mi, it reaches another campsite, and at 2.6 mi it ends at a trail jct. where the loop around the pond began.

❋ Trail in winter: Suitable for snowshoeing and skiing, with one steep hill.

🐾 Distances: Putnam Pond State Campground road to plank bridge, 1.0 mi; to Lost Pond, 1.4 mi; to boulders, 2.0 mi; complete loop around pond, 2.6 mi (4.3 km).

(50) Pharaoh Lake via Mill Brook

Trails Illustrated Map #743: Q28

This is the easiest and most popular trail into the Pharaoh Lake Wilderness from the S. The trail is a nice walk directly to the S end of Pharaoh Lake, from where there is access to the rest of the Pharaoh region via the Pharaoh Mt. trail (trail 40) and the East Shore trail (51).

▶ Trailhead: From Exit 25 on I-87 (the Adirondack Northway), head E on NY 8 to the NE end of Brant Lake. After following the main part of the lake, take the first L (N) onto Palisades Rd. (around the N end of the lake), 0.0 mi. After passing a nice old stone barn on the L at a L bend in the road, and then the Point O' Pines Farm Rd. soon after on the R, take the next R at 1.5 mi onto Beaver Pond Rd. At 2.6 mi, on a bend, the dirt Pharaoh Lake Rd. cuts off to the R. At 3.1 mi, the road reaches the wilderness boundary and a parking lot. From this point the DEC considers this road closed to vehicular traffic, but access is not denied. At some time in the future, this point may be the trailhead. It is another 1.1 mi over a very rough road to the trailhead at Mill Brook. This last section of the road is not plowed in the winter. ◀

FROM THE MILL BROOK PARKING LOT (0.0 mi), the trail heads N across Mill Brook on a nice plank bridge; however, the open area on the other side of Mill Brook may often be flooded with knee-deep water for about 300 ft. The trail register (which is sometimes missing) is in the woods along the trail just after the wet area ends. The trail soon follows an old tote road on a gradual grade NE through attractive woods. At 1.2 mi, the trail bears R and crosses a bridge over a stream. A spur before the bridge to the L leads to an evergreen knoll with an informal campsite that overlooks the beaver pond and large wetland. After crossing the bridge the trail swings L and uphill on the tote road again, with occasional views of Pharaoh Mt. to the N. At 2.0 mi, the road begins descending, soon joining a stream on the L.

An unmaintained footpath enters on the R at 2.4 mi. To the L but poorly marked at this point is the end of the Sucker Brook Trail (trail 55) from Adirondack. The footbridge at the outlet of Pharaoh Lake is reached at 2.5 mi. The Sucker Brook Trail spur foot trail intersects just beyond the bridge. This is also the intersection with the Pharaoh Mt. Trail (trail 40) and the East Shore trail (51).

✳ Trail in winter: Flat, wide, and excellent for skiing and snow-shoeing.

⚹ Distance: Mill Brook to bridge and campsite spur, 1.2 mi; to Pharaoh Lake outlet trail, 2.5 mi (4.0 km).

(51) **East Shore of Pharaoh Lake**

Trails Illustrated Map #743: R28–29

This is a fine trail along the E shore of Pharaoh Lake with some great views of the lake and the surrounding mountains. It passes by three lean-tos and the trails to Whortleberry Pond (trail 54) and Springhill Ponds (trail 52). It's also the connector trail between Mill Brook and the Putnam Pond and Crane Pond area via the Grizzle Ocean Trail (trail 47) and the Glidden Marsh trail (41).

▶ Trailhead: The trail starts at the jct. with the Mill Brook trail (50) and the Pharaoh Mt. Trail (trail 40) by the outlet bridge at the S end of Pharaoh Lake. The trail is marked with yellow markers. ◀

FROM THE TRAIL JCT. (0.0 mi), the trail goes uphill to the R, crossing the clearing and into the woods on the E side of the lake. At 0.4 mi, Lean-to #1 is on the lakeside. From the lean-to are nice views across the lake to Treadway Mt. At the top of the hill beyond the lean-to on the main trail on the R side is the unmaintained side trail for Whortleberry Pond (trail 54).

The trail soon crosses open bedrock with bracken, blueberry bushes, reindeer moss, and trailing arbutus. At 0.7 mi., Lean-to #2 is set back in the woods on the L.

The trail is now narrow and alluring with views of the lake and Pharaoh Mt. In a short distance, at 0.8 mi, the cutoff for Springhill Ponds (trail 52) is on the R. Bear L to continue around the shore of the lake. In about 500 ft, the trail reaches a spur to a small point on the lake. Lean-to #3 used to be here, but has been moved over a mile farther along the trail.

The main trail heads R and soon crosses a couple of rocky bluffs with nice views across the lake. After climbing over a huge rock, the trail drops and crosses a bridge. Soon after going along another high bluff that faces a cove and some islands, the trail reaches another promontory at 1.3 mi. From this point there is a beautiful panorama of the lake, the islands, and the surrounding mountains. The trail then enters a woods of cedars, hemlocks, and pines. After contouring along a steep hillside with red pines, the trail reaches an informal path to Lean-to #3 on the L at a point at 1.9 mi. There's good swimming and great views of the lake and surrounding mountains from the ledge beyond the lean-to.

Turning R, the trail follows a large bay, crosses an inlet, and then wanders through some boulders. After crossing a rocky stream near the shoreline, it crosses the bridge over the outlet from Wolf Pond at 2.3 mi. From here there's a fine view of Wintergreen Point across the water lily-filled bay. At 2.4 mi the trail reaches its N end at the jct. with the Glidden Marsh Trail (trail 41) straight ahead and the Grizzle Ocean Trail (trail 47) on the R.

🦌 Distances: Outlet at S end of Pharaoh Lake to Lean-to #1, 0.4 mi; to Springhill Ponds Trail (trail 52), 0.8 mi; to Glidden Marsh trail (41) and Grizzle Ocean Trail (trail 47) at NE end of Pharaoh Lake, 2.4 mi (3.8 km).

(52) Springhill Ponds

Trails Illustrated Map #743: Q–R29

Springhill Ponds is an interesting destination and a desirable one for those who wish a bit more solitude than the usually popular Pharaoh Lake area affords. The round trip from the Pharaoh Rd. parking lot at Mill Brook is 15.4 mi, so it is not a casual or late-start trip. It would be more feasible for a party camped at one of the Pharaoh Lake lean-tos or as a camping destination itself. Hikers should be prepared for wet going in many places and occasional overgrown sections. With less human presence, opportunities for observing wildlife are much improved and signs of their activity are more evident than in the Pharaoh Lake vicinity.

▶ Trailhead: The Springhill Ponds trail departs R from the yellow-marked trail around the E shore of Pharaoh Lake (trail 51), 0.8 mi from the outlet bridge (and 3.3 mi from the trail register at Mill Brook), by Lean-to #2 near the lake. ◀

LEAVING THE EAST SHORE of Pharaoh Lake trail (51), the trail is initially well marked with red markers. It zigzags around in an E direction to find the driest ground. After 0.2 mi, the trail crosses a small stream and starts to ascend. At this point it is a wide path through an attractive hemlock forest and shows few signs of heavy use by man or beast.

Continuing to ascend, the trail now enters a shallow divide with a rock outcropping on the R. At 0.5 mi, it reaches a height of land and a wet area. The trail is now harder to follow. Bear along the L side among the rocks. Soon afterward it begins a gradual descent through deciduous growth, still traveling E. When leaf cover is light the rocky bulk of Thunderbolt Mt. is visible through the trees, slightly to the L.

After 1.0 mi, the trail enters a glen of conifers where new growth narrows the path, giving it a more intimate feel. Soon afterwards, it crosses a stream and turns to the SE. It now climbs steeply but briefly above the stream and resumes an E direction.

In a now familiar pattern, the trail once again descends to a wet area. It edges around to the S and at 1.5 mi crosses the largest stream since leaving Pharaoh Lake. In spring or other wet periods, the crossing may result in wet feet. Easier crossing is to be found downstream rather than upstream.

Leaving the stream, the trail ascends gently, going from evergreens into a mature deciduous growth. Occasionally the open rocks along the length of Thunderbolt Mt. can be seen more closely to the NE.

The trail has been showing progressively less and less usage and by now the secondary growth is often waist-high and footsteps less secure. After climbing gradually for some distance, the trail enters a cozy glen of hemlocks and a shallow depression. It emerges at a large bog and follows its R bank. The going is level now and offers easy and soft travel over pine needles.

Leaving the bog, the trail parallels a nice feeder stream on the L at roughly 2.1 mi. Several rocks offer good resting spots with the murmur of the stream as background music. Continuing S, the path again becomes quite overgrown. At 2.7 mi, it passes through a cut made in a fallen tree. The walking becomes more level now and, unfortunately, wetter. As the trail climbs slightly, a stream enters from the L and crosses the trail.

Not long afterward the sound of a larger stream is heard. Follow it upstream to the E. The route is now on an old road, which becomes gullied ascending to a crossing with a small set of falls on Spuytenduivel Brook. At 3.5 mi, the path is narrow again and ascends quite steeply from the brook, with thick undergrowth. At the top, the trail is quite indistinct. Turn R and cross a feeder stream. The path bears L shortly and passes through another wet area where trail markers are few and far between amid much low growth.

Turning R and due E, the trail follows a washed-out roadbed steadily uphill and reaches the turn-off for Springhill Ponds on the L (N) at 4.0 mi. The yellow trail to West Hague Rd. (trail 54) goes straight ahead here.

The remaining 0.4 mi to Springhill Ponds involves three more stream crossings, the last being the hardest. Looking upstream from the last one, a very large beaver dam can be seen. After a final rise, the trail descends to the SE shore of the larger Springhill Pond at 4.4 mi. A smaller pond is to the E. An informal fisherman's trail continues around the E shore. On its W end, an attractive rocky promontory with pines overlooks the pond.

🐾 Distances: Pharaoh Lake to small stream, 0.2 mi; to large stream, 1.5 mi; to falls on Spuytenduivel Brook, 3.5 mi; to Springhill Ponds from the South Trail (trail 53), 4.0 mi; to larger Springhill Pond, 4.4 mi (7.0 km). Distance from Pharaoh Rd. parking lot at Mill Brook to Springhill Pond, 7.7 mi (12.9 km).

(53) Springhill Ponds from the South

Trails Illustrated Map #743: Q29–30

This is a new trail which branches from the Berrymill Flow from the South trail (48A). There is a maze of old logging roads near its start, so be certain to keep your eyes on the yellow trail markers. At its W end, it joins the red-marked trail from Pharoah Lake to Springhill Ponds (trail 52) to reach these secluded bodies of water.

▶ Trailhead: At 0.3 mi on the Berrymill Flow from the South trail (48A). ◀

LEAVING TRAIL 48A (0.0 mi) to the L at a "Wilderness Area" sign, the yellow-marked trail narrows and parallels a brook to the R and then crosses it on mossy rocks at 0.5 mi. Crossing several smaller water-courses, the trail becomes brushier and continues steadily uphill with orange survey ribbons (November 2003) along with the yellow markers.

The trail follows a ridge and crosses a small grassy knoll at 1.4 mi and a moss-covered rock face on the R. Watch carefully for trail markers along this twisty section before descending slightly to join a narrow woods road at 2.3 mi. Bear to the R (the L heads to private land), up and over the ridge to the jct. with the red trail from Pharoah Lake at 2.7 mi. The yellow trail ends here as the route forks R, following the red markers to the Springhill ponds (see trail 52).

❄ Trail in winter: Suitable for snowshoeing; skiing would be quite viable except on the middle twisty and steep sections.

🐾 Distances: Trail 48A to grassy knoll and rock face, 1.4 mi; to fork with narrow road, 2.3 mi; to jct. with red trail (trail 52), 3.0 mi (4.8 km). Continuation to Springhill Ponds via trail 52, 3.4 mi (5.5 km).

(54) Whortleberry Pond

Trails Illustrated Map #743: Q28–29

▶ Trailhead: The path begins on the East Shore of Pharaoh Lake trail (51) 120 ft E of a lean-to on the L and privy on the R at the loop trail's 0.4 mi mark. The Whortleberry Pond Trail turns R (S) off the loop trail; coming from the E, one can see a yellow painted arrow on a hemlock at the start of the path; there are occasional faint yellow paint blazes along it. The large hemlocks have carpeted the forest floor with their needles, so there is no underbrush. This trail is not maintained by DEC, but is easy to follow. ◀

LEAVING THE EAST SHORE TRAIL (0.0 mi), at 0.2 mi the route turns R above the pond, reaching an inlet brook. Turn L here and follow the trail along the inlet and through the woods to the water's edge at 0.3 mi. Hemlocks and white pines line the shore. A lovely point across the pond on the E side has a bog on its N side. A great blue heron, crows, bluejays, ravens, chickadees, and woodpeckers are among the resident species. Stevens Mt. (elev. 2103 ft) and Little Stevens Mt. are visible S. Bushwhacking is not difficult in these open woods. This secluded pond is a birdwatcher's paradise.

🐾 Distance: East Shore of Pharaoh Lake trail (51) to Whortleberry Pond, 0.3 mi (0.5 km).

(55) Sucker Brook and Desolate Brook Trail to Pharaoh Lake

Trails Illustrated Map #743: Q–R27

▶ Trailhead: From the Adirondack General Store in the town of Adirondack on the E shore of Schroon Lake, drive E 0.5 mi on Beaver Pond Rd. to a large sign for the Pharaoh Lake Horse Trail. Turn L at the sign, drive 0.2 mi to a T, then L again for 0.6 mi to a parking lot at a dead end. This is a horse trail marked with yellow markers. A long, remote trail, it may be difficult to follow. ◀

AN OLD ROAD leaves the Pharaoh Lake Horse Trail parking lot (0.0 mi) and rises gently, heading N through beautiful woods. At 0.9 mi, the road crosses a stream. Then it goes through a cedar grove. Another small stream intersects the road at 1.0 mi, and another at 1.3 mi. At 1.4 mi, another old road enters on the L. Continuing straight ahead, the road steadily climbs at a gentle grade.

At 1.6 mi, an old driveway goes up to the R with a stone wall opposite. On the R is the foundation of a farmhouse with a deep cellar. Now the road goes down again. At 1.7 mi and 2.1 mi it crosses streams.

A beaver pond is visible down to the L at 2.5 mi. It is interesting to walk downhill through the woods over an old dump of bottles, cans, and an old cast iron stove to get a better look at the pond. A huge beaver house is along the close shore to the L. This pond is a wide place in Sucker Brook.

Now the old road ends and walking becomes more difficult after a R turn (E) to follow the pass that Sucker Brook flows through. It is necessary to thread your way through the woods on a narrow trail that crosses Sucker Brook at 2.6 mi and again at 2.7 mi, then winds up and over the N side of Orange Hill. At 2.9 mi, the trail starts down again, then up and downhill some more. At 3.3 mi, it crosses Sucker Brook again, generally following the valley of the brook.

At 4.7 mi, the trail makes the first of several turns down the N side of No. 8 Hill, first R, then L, until crossing Desolate Brook at 5.0 mi.

At 5.1 mi, the trail crosses another branch of Desolate Brook, aptly named, for these are dark, dank woods. Huge hemlocks and maples tower above. A carpet of bunchberry covers the barely discernible trail. At 5.4 mi, it climbs a short hill, with the brook occasionally visible, winding a sinuous course down to the L.

At 5.6 mi, the trail turns R and at 5.8 mi climbs around a low shoulder on the SW side of Pharaoh Mt. At 6.1 mi it starts downhill, crossing a muck hole and climbing briefly before beginning a steep descent through beech woods. The trail crosses a small brook at 6.4 mi in a level stretch among incredibly tall, straight trees.

In the next 0.5 mi the trail crosses several small streams. At 7.1 mi, it goes more steeply uphill, soon leveling out. At 7.4 mi, the trail becomes an old road going downhill to a clearing. The horse trail goes R and then L to a wet crossing of Pharaoh Lake Brook. It meets the Mill Brook trail (50) at 7.5 mi. On trail 50 it is a few hundred feet L to the picturesque outlet of Pharaoh Lake, the first long-distance view of the trip, and an intersection with the Pharaoh Mt. Trail (trail 40) and the East Shore trail (51).

A drier crossing of Pharaoh Lake Brook is possible via the foot trail spur at a L turn in the clearing at 7.4 mi. It is a short distance to the bridge on the spillway at the Pharaoh Lake outlet.

A good cross-country ski run would be a trip on the old road from Adirondack to the beaver pond, a round trip of 5.1 mi.

⚹ Distances: To cellar hole, 1.6 mi; to beaver pond, 2.5 mi; to No. 8 Hill, 4.7 mi; to Mill Brook trail (50) and Pharaoh Lake, 7.5 mi (12.1 km). To parking lot at Mill Brook, 10.1 mi (16.9 km).

(56) Spectacle Pond

Trails Illustrated Map #743: R27

This is a beautiful and relaxing walk in deep woods.

▶ Trailhead: From I-87 (Adirondack Northway) Exit 25 (Chestertown–Hague) turn E onto NY 8, then L (N) immediately after the northbound entrance ramp at a brown and yellow sign for Adirondack. After 8.0 mi, turn L at a T then take the first R at Adirondack General Store. After 5.0 mi there are State Forest Preserve signs on trees. After another mile there is a wide turn-out on the R for the trailhead. A sign says Spectacle Pond, 2.0 mi. Actually, the walk is a little shorter, at 1.7 mi. ◀

THERE IS A YELLOW DEC TRAIL SIGN here at the start of this old logging road (0.0 mi), which bends L. At 0.1 mi the trail crosses Spectacle Brook on a bridge. At the end of May there is a profusion of wildflowers in these rich woods: ladyslippers, foamflower, *clintonia borealis*, jack-in-the-pulpit, and violets. At 0.2 mi, the trail crosses a second bridge over the stream and at 0.5 mi a third bridge.

At 0.6 mi, the trail begins to climb. The stream provides a pleasant companion with its many small cascades, twists, and turns around moss-covered rocks. At 0.9 mi, the trail crosses a small stream. At 1.0 mi, it passes a wetland, then turns L at 1.2 mi and reaches the foot of Spectacle Pond at 1.3 mi.

At 1.4 mi, the trail comes to beaver dams above and below a bridge over the outlet of the pond. After crossing the bridge, the trail turns L and follows a ridge that ends as a rocky promontory in the pond at 1.7 mi, giving an excellent view of Pharaoh Mt.

🚶 Distances: Trailhead to third bridge, 0.5 mi; to foot of Spectacle Pond, 1.3 mi; to promontory, 1.7 mi (2.9 km).

(57) Gull Pond

Trails Illustrated Map #743: R27

▶ Trailhead: Drive N from the Adirondack General Store (see trail 56) 7.1 mi. This is 1.1 mi N of the trailhead for Spectacle Pond (trail 56). The trailhead parking area for Gull Pond is off the road on the R. ◀

FROM THE PARKING AREA (0.0 mi), the trail goes through deep woods, wet in places, until it climbs a rocky outcrop overlooking Gull Pond at 0.5 mi. This is a jewel of a pond with sheer rock cliffs across on the E side. There are blueberry bushes on the rocks. No camping is permitted at the lookout.

🚶 Distance: Trailhead parking lot to Gull Pond, 0.5 mi (0.8 km).

(58) Severance Mt.

Trails Illustrated Map #743: S26–27

▶ Trailhead: Drive 0.6 mi S of I-87 (Adirondack Northway) Exit 28 on NY 9. Turn R into a large parking lot on two levels—with a hitching post for each car. The lot is clearly marked with a large sign for Severance Mt. by the road. ◀

IMMEDIATELY BEYOND THE PARKING LOT (0.0 mi), two long culverts carry the trail under the N and S lanes of the Northway. The trail ducks into the woods at 0.1 mi, following yellow trail markers. The path is wide and starts to go up at 0.2 mi. The grade becomes steeper at 0.3

mi. The trail climbs steadily through mixed woods of maple, white pine, birch, hemlock, and white cedar. Unfortunately, the noise of traffic on the Northway is quite loud. Soon the trail takes a sharp turn R, avoiding an old logging road to the S side of the trail.

At 0.5 mi, the trail levels off. At 0.6 mi it crosses two plank bridges and then at 0.7 mi another plank bridge over the same small stream. Now the sound of traffic is faint. The trail begins to climb again, at 0.8 mi, winding on the level through a lovely hemlock grove. Then after a large boulder on the L at 0.9 mi, the trail climbs again. At 1.0 mi, it winds uphill through beech and hemlock woods.

At 1.2 mi, the trail reaches an overlook with a view of Schroon Lake and Pharaoh Mt. to the E. A second overlook about 100 ft farther overlooks Paradox Lake. The rest of the summit is covered with trees. Curious ravens with beady eyes often swoop over the treetops, then perform their feats of skydiving skill in front of the cliff directly below. A DEC sign says the ascent is 813 ft, but the USGS map shows about 700 ft of ascent from the parking lot to the summit.

❊ Trail in winter: This is a pleasant snowshoe in winter and a nice trip for good skiers (intermediate and better).

🐾 Distance: Trailhead to plank bridges, 0.6 mi; to summit, 1.2 mi (2.0 km). Ascent, 700 ft (213 m). Summit elevation, 1638 ft.

(59) Cook Mt.

Trails Illustrated Map #743: R31–32

This is the northernmost climb in the Lake George Basin region. From the top are views S to Anthonys Nose, Lake George, and Rogers Rock, with Black Mt. and the Tongue Mt. Range off in the distance. To the E is Mt. Defiance, with Lake Champlain and the Green Mountains beyond. The Cook Mt. Preserve is owned and maintained by the Lake George Basin Land Conservancy and is open to the public for recreational, educational, and scientific purposes. For more information, please contact them at PO Box 1250, Bolton Landing, NY 12814, phone 518-644-9673.

▶ Trailhead: Approximately 1.0 mi S of the monument and traffic circle in Ticonderoga on NY 9N, turn E onto Essex Co. Rte. 5. At about 1.2 mi, turn R (S) onto Baldwin Rd. The trailhead is 1.5 mi S on Baldwin Rd. on the R at a gate on an old logging road with L.G. Basin Land Conservancy signs. Just beyond on the L is a state historical marker referring to this area as "Abercrombie's landing, where 15,000 men landed to attack Ticonderoga which was successfully defended by Montcalm in July 1758." ◀

FROM THE GATE (0.0 mi), the trail follows a grassy old road W toward Cook Mt. In just 0.1 mi a very active beaver flow with several ponds and lodges is on the R. Branches of the trail go on either side of the flow, meeting on the far side. The road soon turns L (S) and begins climbing. At 0.3 mi, it turns R at a Y and then R again at the next intersection.

In a short distance, an unmarked path leads to the L. Stay straight ahead on the old road, until at 0.5 mi, the trail, marked with red markers, heads sharply L at a sign that says Summit Trail.

From here the well-marked trail climbs at a steady pace up terrain that varies from gradually to moderately steep, ascending a series of small ridges up the side of the mountain through a lovely open hardwood forest of oak, beech, and maple. At 0.8 mi, the trail joins what appears to be an old logging road and turns R (NW), then soon heads more westerly again. A level plateau is at 1.0 mi, but the trail soon swings L with some rock cairns near a posted private land boundary.

Climbing moderately again, the trail reaches an open area at 1.2 mi. It's pretty here with a variety of mosses, junipers, and pines, and a view to the N above the trees. Before reaching the S end of this open area, the trail takes a sharp L into the woods. From here the hiking is much more gradual. Climbing over a series of small ledges, the trail turns to the R and proceeds in a SE direction up over more small ledges.

The rocky top is at 1.3 mi, with the trail marked mostly by rock cairns. Here there are great views to the S and E above the scrub oaks. The trail continues S across the rock toward the main part of Lake George, descending gently on an almost indistinct path with red markers, then soon turns R in a more SW direction at 1.4 mi, to a small open ledge S at about 1.7 mi. For the adventurous, the reward is a great outlook over the entire N Lake George basin, with nice views to the E from the open rocky areas along the way. There should be lots of blueberries in season.

✳ Trail in winter: With adequate snow cover, this is a great snowshoe, though rather steep in a few spots. Snowshoe crampons are recommended. Views are great without leaves on the trees.

🐾 Distances: Baldwin Rd. to Summit Trail sign, 0.5 mi; to high point,

105

1.3 mi; to open ledge at S end of summit, 1.7 mi (2.7 km). Ascent from Baldwin Rd., 895 ft (273 m). Elevation, 1230 ft (375 m).

(60) **Rogers Rock**

Trails Illustrated Map #743: Q–R31

This is a short hike with a very steep trail, so it is not recommended for small children. The view is spectacular.

▶ Trailhead: From the village of Hague on Lake George, drive N on NY 9N 4.0 mi to Rogers Rock State Campground. There is also a beach and boat launch site here. There is a day-use fee in spring, summer, and fall. ◀

After the entrance booth, take a sharp L and drive 1.2 mi to a turn-off on the L for campsites. The trail starts at campsite 210. There is no sign, and the trail is not marked or maintained by DEC.

FROM CAMPSITE 210 (0.0 mi), a small, well-defined path climbs gradually past a Private Land sign on a tree, through hemlock, pine, and oak woods. At 0.2 mi it turns L (N) at a boulder slope and follows a small gully along the base of the mountain. At the top of the gully by a boulder on the L, the trail angles R up the face of the mountain. At 0.3 mi, it climbs up a steep ledge.

The first view opens as the trail continues up steeply, with Cooks Bay below on Lake George. From 0.5 mi to 0.7 mi there is a succession of fantastic views along the ridge and, in summer, plenty of blueberries. Now the trail ducks into oak and white pine woods. In season, pale corydalis blooms in the shallow soil on top of the rock shelf. At 0.9 mi, the trail reaches another outlook, then descends to an open rock face at 1.0 mi. Continue along this rock until the end of the trail at 1.1 mi. It is possible to walk a little farther, but trees obstruct the view and then there is no further passage.

There is a maze of paths across the broad summit N and E of the lookouts. If you try these paths, head W on them until you reach the steep, rocky scramble you came up. Robert Rogers struggled to put on his snowshoes backwards near here and then beat a hasty retreat, successfully fooling the Indians pursuing him. They concluded from the snowshoe tracks that Rogers had fallen to his death over the cliff.

From this perch one can see E to Vermont, S down Lake George, and W to the southern Adirondacks. Along the E shore of Lake George are

View of Lake George from Rogers Rock. CARL HEILMAN II

Anthonys Nose jutting into the lake, Record Hill, South Mt., Spruce Mt., Elephant Mt., and Black Mt.

❋ Trail in winter: This is a steep trail, even for snowshoes. The snow can often be crusted or icy so it's important to have crampons on the snowshoes, or to be able to switch over to just crampons.

❧ Distances: Campsite 210 to steep ledge, 0.3 mi; to level ridge, 0.5 mi; to Rogers Rock, 1.1 mi (1.8 km). Elevation of Rogers Rock, 1027 ft (313 m). ♦

Lake George and French Point Mt. JAMES APPLEYARD

Northwestern Lake George Wild Forest Section

This region is a fairly extensive area with a combination of old roads and some motorized access, and some fine hiking trails. It is bounded by NY 8 on the N, US 9 on the W, and the Warrensburg/Diamond Point area on the S. The shoreline of Lake George forms the E boundary. Along this section of Lake George is the Tongue Mt. Range and some great hiking, with fine views looking into the wildest parts of the lake. While parts of the Tongue Mt. Range are heavily used, more isolated areas, both on Tongue Mt. and in the rest of this region, see very minimal use through the year. Access to some of the region is over very messy 4WD roads, which diminishes the experience at the destination. A number of the roads in this region head toward good fishing ponds and are great for portaging in a small ultralight canoe. While some of the snowmobile trails are suggested as foot trails, these trails are maintained for winter use and may be quite wet at some times in the spring, summer, and fall, particularly since they are used by ATVs. Trash dumping has gone along with this use, further degrading the setting. Since this is a Wild Forest area, these roads can also be used for mountain biking. Many of them are rather rough and unimproved, so expect a good challenge, not a groomed surface.

The Tongue Mt. area is home to the endangered eastern timber rattlesnake. The snakes are not aggressive and are seldom seen; however, please observe the cautions in the trail descriptions that mention the snakes and remember that this is their home, not ours.

❋ Trails in winter: This region has some nice skiing and snowshoeing possibilities. Most trails, with the exception of the Tongue Mt. region, are great for skiing when there's adequate snow. There is snowmobiling on some of the old roads, and there are snowmobile routes through the region, so you may not have the trail to yourself. These routes, though, are not too heavily used, except sometimes on holiday weekends. Some fresh powder on top of a packed snowmobile trail can make for fine skiing.

The whole Tongue Mt. area is too rugged for skiing, but there's some good snowshoeing over the mountains. Be sure to carry crampons for poor snow conditions and ice.

Suggested hikes in the region:

SHORT HIKE:
• Deer Leap—1.1 mi (1.8 km) from the Tongue Mt. trailhead to an overlook above Lake George. This is a heavily traveled trail because it is near the road, with views of the lake at the end.

MODERATE HIKE:
• Northwest Bay Trail—5.0 mi (8.7 km) one way. Very pretty and mostly flat along the shoreline. One may hike as far as one chooses and then return to the trailhead.

HARDER HIKE:
• Tongue Mt. Traverse—11.8 mi (17.9 km). From NY 9N on the N to Montcalm Point on the S, this is one of the most strenuous and spectacular routes in the eastern Adirondacks. With the Fifth Peak lean-to midway, this can be a fine backpacking trip, or a one-day trip. It's possible to be picked up by boat from Montcalm Point, or one can return to the Clay Meadows trailhead via the Northwest Bay trail for a total of 16.2 mi.

(61) Lily Pond from Grassville Rd. to NY 8

Trails Illustrated Map #743: O28

This route is a nice walk, and a great ski in the winter, especially when it's linked with further exploration to Round Pond and Buttermilk Pond via the Round, Duck, and Buttermilk Ponds trail (62). Some sections of this route are old town roads, open to automobiles, while other sections are snowmobile trails closed to all other motorized vehicles. The area is in theory not traveled by ATVs, though, on busy weekends. It's also a great route for an adventurous mountain biker.

There are plans to upgrade the road into Lily Pond, so this area may see more traffic. The State is currently (2005) trying to close off this abuse with a lawsuit in the State Supreme Court asking that motorized access be stopped. DEC has suspended enforcement against ATV riders pending the outcome of this case. Road closure is an outcome devoutly to be wished, and restoration would take at least a decade of cleanup by Mother Nature and her offspring.

This description proceeds from the highest trailhead (S) to the lowest for the benefit of skiers.

▶ Trailhead: From the Horicon Fire Dept. (0.0 mi) in the town of Brant Lake, follow NY 8 E. At 2.3 mi, turn R (S) onto Grassville Rd. At 1.0 mi, follow the road sharp R. At 1.9 mi, the road becomes dirt. A small camp and clearing are at 3.0 mi. If parking on the private land just past the camp, be sure to ask permission, or park just along the road. It may be better to park along the wider section of road just before reaching the camp. This is the S access. ◀

The unmarked N trailhead along NY 8 is 3.7 mi beyond Grassville Rd. (6.0 mi from the Horicon Fire Dept.). After an S-turn on NY 8 with a 25 MPH suggested speed limit, the dirt road to Lily Pond is on the R, just before a fair-sized stream. On the L (N) are cabins on the shore of Brant Lake. The camp named Tak-it-E-Z is just beyond the access road on the L (N), and 0.3 mi past it is Palisades Rd. on the L (N), which winds around the N shoreline of Brant Lake. A small gray garage is on the R (S) side of NY 8, just to the L of the road to Lily Pond. At some time a small parking lot may be built here, but at present (2005), parking is on the shoulder of NY 8.

FROM THE CLEARING, just beyond the camp (0.0 mi), the road heads gradually downhill. In a short distance a small stream crosses. At 0.3 mi, another stream crosses along a rock water bar. At 0.4 mi, a DEC trail marker indicates Grassville Rd. to the L. Avoid the L though, as this travels over private lands back to the sharp R turn on Grassville Rd. Follow to the R for the trail to Lily Pond.

The road climbs gradually uphill, then at 0.6 mi drops back down again on a moderate grade. The keen observer will pick out remnants of the long-abandoned homesteads all through this area. At 0.9 mi, the road begins a long gradual descent, passing a snowmobile trail (a wet route in the summer) to Island Pond on the R (S) at 1.0 mi, and reaching the S shore of Lily Pond at 1.1 mi. Here there is an informal campsite and fire ring at a nice lookout over the pond. Continuing on the road to the E, there is a bridge over an inlet stream, with a lot of beaver activity visible. At a jct. at 1.2 mi, the road to NY 8 heads L (N). The road straight ahead is the Round, Duck, and Buttermilk Ponds trail (62).

Turn L to go along the E shoreline of the lake on the wide path. In a short distance the path splits, then rejoins again soon. The L route more closely follows the shoreline, with some nice views of the pond along the way.

After passing over a couple of informal campsites, the trail joins the dirt road from NY 8 at 1.5 mi. Here it is just about 100 ft to an open area on the L overlooking Lily Pond. The pond is pretty, but the foreground has been littered extensively.

Turning R, the dirt road follows but is out of sight of the E shoreline. At 2.0 mi, it crosses over the outlet of the pond. There has been a lot of beaver activity here in the past, and this section has often been flooded.

The road gradually begins to descend and at 2.3 mi crosses a bridge over the outlet stream, recrossing it again at 2.5 mi, after passing an old beaver pond. At 2.7 mi, the stream may be heard on the R. From here the road drops steadily at a gradual to moderate rate, then reaches a jct. with an old road joining on the L (W) at 3.1 mi. At 3.5 mi, the road descends again, past a yellow Forest Preserve sign on the R, at a moderate rate almost the whole way to the unmarked jct. with NY 8 at 3.8 mi.

❋ Trail in winter: While this route is frequented by snowmobilers, it can be a delightful ski trip. Additional routes can be included by going to Buttermilk Pond or taking the cutoff to Island Pond (a snowmobile trail not described because of its wet character in the summer).

⚹ Distances: Grassville Rd. to jct. L to private lands, 0.4 mi; to first outlook over Lily Pond, 1.1 mi; to the Round, Duck and Buttermilk Ponds trail (62), 1.2 mi; to road to NY 8, 1.5 mi; to Lily Pond outlet, 2.0 mi; to NY 8, 3.8 mi (6.1 km).

(62) Round, Duck, and Buttermilk Ponds

Trails Illustrated Map #743: O–P28

This can be an enjoyable, though sometimes wet, walk (or bike) to a couple of nice fishing ponds in the Brant Lake area. The terrain is rolling, and the route uses mostly old roads in the area. Evidence of ATV use abounds and is testimony to the destructive power of these machines.

▶ Trailhead: This trail begins at the 1.2-mi point on the Lily Pond trail (61) and heads E along the old road. ◀

CONTINUING STRAIGHT AHEAD from the Lily Pond trail (0.0 mi), the road climbs steadily uphill and at 0.1 mi reaches a jct. The L fork is the Buttermilk Loop Trail (trail 62A), a pleasant alternative route to Buttermilk Pond; it rejoins trail 62 and is described below as part of the return loop in this description. To skip Round and Duck ponds for a slightly shorter and drier hike, turn L at this fork and take trail 62A only to Buttermilk Pond.

Continuing straight ahead, the road is now marked with orange DEC snowmobile trail disks. At 0.3 mi, a small stream which the trail crosses on a bridge at 0.4 mi at a wide, shallow place can be heard on the R.

At 0.7 mi, the trail reaches the top of a rise and then starts downhill. At 0.8 mi, it curves L from E to N and goes slightly uphill. At 0.9 mi, it reaches a pile of stones on the L. At 1.0 mi, the road forks L through a very wet intersection. Stay straight.

After climbing, the trail goes downhill again toward Round Pond. At 1.1 mi, the trail makes a sharp curve L. (A foot trail that is unmarked and unmaintained by DEC but has painted blazes on trees heads off to the R.) The trail heads L and downhill, passing the intersection of the cut-off trail which branched L at the wet intersection.

Still winding downhill, the trail arrives at lovely Round Pond at 1.3 mi. This is an attractive pond with some rocky shoreline. Minnows warm themselves in the shallows and giant dragonflies patrol the air. A pair of ravens may come flying and squawking overhead.

A small foot trail slightly L goes on to Duck Pond at 1.5 mi after crossing through muddy ruts and blowdown in a cedar swamp. There is a large flat rock here for a rest and picnic.

Retracing your steps to the jct., turn L at 1.7 mi on another narrow trail marked with snowmobile markers. This leads into a swamp with rotten corduroys. There have been cedars cut (perhaps for a bridge?) near a flooded corduroy with floating logs. It is important to keep watch for the orange snowmobile trail markers since the trail is faint.

At 1.8 mi, the trail crosses a stream on stones. It soon reaches a wooden snowmobile trail sign pointing S.

At the intersection with the snowmobile sign, the route L connects to the trail to Buttermilk Pond. The trail goes through cedars following orange snowmobile trail markers. At 2.4 mi, it reaches open rock with moss, bracken, and young balsam firs. At 2.6 mi, the faint trail is in a low, dark, and wet cedar swamp with a rocky hill on the R. At 2.7 mi, it curves R and into a birch grove. Now the path is barely discernible.

At 2.8 mi, the trail recombines with the Buttermilk Loop Trail (62A). The L route turns NE and then swings SW toward Lily Pond. R is Buttermilk Pond. The snowmobile signs are orange.

The road heads uphill through a pass. At 3.0 mi, the trail reaches a crest. It is growing over with beech and striped maple saplings. Now the trail goes level through huge ferns, birch, beech, and maple. At 3.4 mi, it turns abruptly L after descending from the end of the ridge, and then crosses a stream. Now it turns sharply R downhill along the stream.

The trail passes two small ponds R and leads through a glade of hay-scented ferns. At 3.7 mi, Buttermilk Pond can be seen ahead, and moments later the trail reaches the S end of the pond. To the L is an unmarked ATV path along the shore. At 3.8 mi there is a huge beaver lodge along the shore. A small point to the L with huge white pines and a large rocky bluff on the opposite shore make this a picturesque and peaceful spot.

❋ Trail in winter: Suitable for snowshoeing and cross country skiing, but snowmobile use may be heavy.

❀ Distances: To W end of Buttermilk Loop Trail (trail 62A), 0.1 mi; to Round Pond, 1.3 mi; to Duck Pond, 1.5 mi; to E end of Buttermilk Loop Trail, 2.8 mi; to Buttermilk Pond, 3.8 mi (6.1 km).

(62A) Buttermilk Loop Trail

Trails Illustrated Map #743: O–P28

This trail is an "express" route to Buttermilk Pond, bypassing Round and Duck Ponds. Because it provides a variation on the return hike from Buttermilk Pond, it is described here in that direction (E to W).

▶ Trailheads: Interior trail, with trailheads at 0.1 mi (W end) and 2.8 mi (E end) on the Round, Duck, and Buttermilk Ponds trail (62). The trail is described from E to W. ◀

AN UNNAMED POND glistens on the R just before the E trailhead. Just past this jct., where there is bare rock for the roadbed (a pleasure after several miles of faint and wet trails), one can walk 300 ft to the R on a small trail to the edge of this pond. Brush around the edge obscures the view, but it might be a good place to fish.

The trail, in fact an old road, heads first NW (there are pink ladys-lippers here in early June) and then SW through lovely woods. It is marked with yellow snowmobile markers and is a bit less marred by the ruts from 4WD vehicles than is trail 62. At 0.8 mi, the road is bare rock after passing a square stone foundation R.

At 1.0 mi, the road crosses a bridge of stone slabs and goes through an old farm clearing with an apple tree. The walking is level. At 1.9 mi, the road passes a large old apple tree and then a pile of rocks on the L. At 2.1 mi, it rejoins Round, Duck, and Buttermilk Ponds trail (62). Turn R here to reach the Lily Pond trail (61) in 0.1 mi.

❋ Trail in winter: Suitable for cross country skiing and snowshoeing.

❀ Distance: E trailhead to stone slab bridge, 1.0 mi; to W trailhead, 2.1 mi (3.4 km).

(63) **Long and Island Ponds**

Trails Illustrated Map #743: O28

Long Pond is a good fishing spot, but swimming is not recommended because of leeches. They range in size from 1/16 inch to 5 inches and are quick to establish a relationship. The pond is used mostly by anglers. Beavers are quite active here. A short connector trail leads from Long Pond to Island Pond, where in winter a snowmobile trail leads from the NW corner of the pond up to Lily Pond.

▶ Trailhead: From Brant Lake Fire Station, drive E 1.7 mi on NY 8 to Duell Hill Rd. on the R. Turn up this steep road and continue on it for 3.1 mi, passing Orin Duell Rd., Jim Youngs Rd., Streeter Pond Rd., Harris Rd., and Granger Rd. Now turn L. This is called the Padanarum Spur Rd. After 1.0 mi, the road reaches a green camp called "Cirlew." Here the road turns to a narrow track that is not maintained from December 1 to April 1. Continue another 0.8 mi down this narrow dirt track to the trailhead for Long Pond on the L. (0.0 mi.) It is an old road going uphill at a white and green ATV sign with an arrow. Further up this hill is an orange DEC snowmobile disk, a trail sign for the two ponds, and a DEC fishing sign. The regulatory confusion is compounded by a sign prohibiting ATV use on this trail, a rule which is being blatantly ignored, as the condition of the old road attests. There is a small space to park on the R just beyond the turnoff. ◀

FROM THE TRAILHEAD (0.0 mi), the old road on the L (N) goes straight uphill along a washed-out section for 0.1 mi. The trail levels out, then there is a series of huge mud holes made by vehicles. At 0.3 mi, a new wide side trail has been cut on the L around a large wet area, the first of several similar detours.

At 0.5 mi, the road descends gently to another wet spot, then climbs into pines. At 0.8 mi, it goes up, then at 0.9 mi levels off in birch, white pine, hemlock, balsam, and maple woods.

At 1.0 mi, the road curves L 90 degrees. At 1.1 mi, there is a trail sign L to Island Pond (see below). The R fork leads in 0.1 mi to the S end of Long Pond, after a descent of 250 ft. Beavers have raised the pond level considerably. There is an informal campsite here.

The continuation to Island Pond is pleasant but sometimes wet, first along a ridge and then in and out of ferns. At 1.5 mi, it reaches a flooded edge of pretty Island Pond, which seems to be completely filled in, perhaps the work of beavers. Both ponds are fun to explore in a small ultralight canoe.

🛶 Distances: Padanarum Spur Rd. to Long Pond spur, 1.1 mi; to Island Pond, 1.5 mi (2.4 km). Round trip spur to Long Pond, 0.2 mi.

(64) **Wardsboro Rd. from N to S**
(64A) **Wardsboro Rd. Side Trail**

Trails Illustrated Map #743: P29–30

This trail follows an old road that passes through some nice wild land in the NE part of this region. The N section travels through some private lands, including some timber lands, but there is a public easement to use the road. Approximately the first half mile has been built up to a hard road surface for logging trucks, but the road becomes more of a trail after this. This is a great route for skiing (park a car at both the N and S ends of the trail). There no longer is public access to Swede Pond or Swede Mt.

▶ Trailhead: The N trailhead is on NY 8, 1.0 mi E of the E end of North Pond (approx. 10 mi E of the firehouse in the town of Brant Lake and about 1.0 mi W of the town of Graphite). Soon after North Pond, a rock painted to resemble an elephant is on the R. A posted logging header is on the R. In about 0.1 mi, take a sharp R onto Fly Brook Rd. Park on the R side of Fly Brook Rd.

To reach the S trailhead, drive 5.0 mi E from I-87 (Adirondack Northway) Exit 24 to NY 9N, then turn L (N) and drive 6.0 mi. to Padanarum Rd. (dirt) on the L. At 1.8 mi, cross a bridge, then turn R onto Wardsboro Rd. and drive to a parking turnout across from a red cabin at 3.4 mi. The old Wardsboro cemetery can be seen here. ◀

FROM THE N TRAILHEAD (0.0 mi), walk along Fly Brook Rd. past an intersection on the R with the gated logging heading. Continue ahead, walking gently uphill to a L (S) turn onto a side road at 0.4 mi. This is the N end of the Wardsboro road.

The logging is soon left behind and the road becomes less rutted. Bear L up the hill, until at 0.9 mi the road reaches the top of the hill and bears R (S). At 1.1 mi, at a fork, the main trail is on the R, while a the Wardsboro Rd. Side Trail (trail 64A) heads to the L see below). Stay on the main trail.

The road soon heads downhill and comes to a stream on the L at 1.6 mi. At 2.2 mi, there is a large detour around a big beaver pond, and a

117

second jct. with trail 64A is at 2.3 mi.

(The Wardsboro Rd. Side Trail [trail 64A] heads L from its N jct. with the main trail [0.0 mi], and descends gradually at first, then more steeply. At 0.4 mi, there is a jct. with an old road on the L. Heading to the R, the road becomes eroded and then soon levels off at 0.7 mi. The road descends again to the jct. with the main trail by the beaver pond at 1.5 mi. It is 0.3 mi longer than the equivalent section of trail 64.)

From the S jct. of trails 64 and 64A, below the beaver pond, the road passes over some rolling terrain with some wet sections and reaches a stream at 2.7 mi. The road varies from level to muddy to rolling, and passes occasional beaver handiwork.

At 3.8 mi, there is another stream crossing. The road descends on a gradual grade and at 4.3 mi reaches a cabin on the L. There are some signs of logging, and then the road descends alongside a hill with a pretty glen down to the L at 4.6 mi.

After a stone bridge over the outlet of Spectacle Ponds, a small green house on the R is at 5.0 mi. At 5.4 mi, orange markers on the trees on the L announce that the stream is a nursery for Atlantic landlocked salmon. The old Wardsboro cemetery is just ahead at 5.6 mi.

🚶 Distances: Parking along Fly Brook Rd. to L turn onto Wardsboro Rd., 0.4 mi; to N jct. with trail 64A, 1.1 mi; to S jct. with 64A, 2.3 mi; to cabin, 4.3 mi; to Wardsboro cemetery, 5.6 mi (9.0 km). Length of trail 64A, 1.5 mi (2.4 km).

(64B) Jabe Pond

Trails Illustrated Map #743: P30

Jabe Pond is a fairly recent addition to the Forest Preserve and has 4WD access.

▶ Trailhead: From NY 9N midway between Hague and Silver Bay, Split Rock Rd. heads W and uphill. At 1.8 mi, Jabe Pond Rd. starts L (S). This dirt road is occasionally maintained and often muddy, with one steep, bumpy hill. Those without 4WD vehicles should perhaps walk the mile to the pond. ◀

THE POND HAS GOOD CANOEING, with a twisty shoreline and islands to explore. It is surrounded by low mountains in a lovely setting. There are designated campsites, and small motors of 10 HP or less are allowed on boats. An old road on the W shore leads to a herd path with Little

Jabe Pond 0.3 mi away.

❋ Trail in winter: Jabe Pond Rd. is not plowed in winter, providing good snowshoe or ski access to the pond.

🐾 Distance: Split Rock Rd. to Jabe Pond, 1.0 mi (1.6 km).

CAT AND THOMAS MT. PRESERVE

Trails Illustrated Map #743: L–M27

This is a new preserve of the Lake George Land Conservancy, and it opened in 2004. It consists of 1900 acres with two summits and rolling land between, W of Bolton Landing on the W shore of Lake George. Much of the land was logged before the establishment of the preserve, so access is by logging roads, on which the three trails are laid out. The preserve protects the watershed of Edgecomb Pond, which is Bolton Landing's drinking water source. There are wonderful views of the S basin of Lake George, and the forest is recovering from the logging.

▶ Trailhead: From I-87 (the Adirondack Northway), take Exit 24 and head E on Co. Rte. 11 for approx. 2.0 mi. Turn R (S) on Valley Woods Rd. The preserve parking lot is almost immediately on the R, with a kiosk and register. ◀

(64C) Thomas Mt. Trail

Trails Illustrated Map #743: M27

THIS IS A 1.5 MI LONG ROAD to an overlook below the top (which is private) of the Thomas Mt. ridge, where there is a small locked cabin and a stupendous view to the S. It is marked with orange disks, with two at each bend and four on a post at the fork with the Cat Mt. Trail (trail 64D, see below).

Heading L (S) from the kiosk and trail register (0.0 mi) past a gate and along a road slightly downhill, the route winds up past a large excavation on the R to a fork in a clearing with a disk-marked post indicating the jct. with the Cat Mt. Trail (trail 64D) at 0.7 mi. Take the R fork uphill steadily to a R hairpin at 1.0 mi. Continuing up the road into the fringe of unlogged hemlock woods, the trail ends at the cabin and lookout on the L at 1.5 mi. The summit is to the N; it is on private land and is not accessible.

❋ Trail in winter: Excellent for snowshoeing and superb for skiing.

🐾 Distances: Kiosk to Cat Mt. Trail (trail 64D), 0.7 mi; to hairpin,

1.0 mi; to cabin and lookout, 1.5 mi (2.4 km). Ascent, 780 ft (238 m). Elevation, 1980 ft (604 m).

(64D) Cat Mt. Trail

Trails Illustrated Map #743: L–M27

THIS STARTS AS A ROLLING ROADWAY, mostly on a sidehill, which runs from the fork and post at 0.7 mi along the Thomas Mt. Trail (trail 64C), past a small pond and to a gate, where it eventually narrows to a trail as it ascends Cat Mt. It is marked with blue markers until it comes to a gate, and then yellow markers to the summit.

At the marked fork on the Thomas Mt. Trail (trail 64C) (0.0 mi), bear L, straight ahead and downhill out of the clearing, following blue markers. This rolling road crosses a small stream, ascends to a clearing, and proceeds to the open shore of a small pond at 1.0 mi. Cat Mt. is visible to the SW over the pond. The trail continues across the outlet of the pond, through a darker hemlock woods, to a gate at 1.3 mi.

Past the gate, the route becomes more of a trail, marked with yellow disks (be alert to the yellow markers; intersecting woods roads can lead you astray). Leaving the gate, the route heads R (W) uphill, then zig-zags down, up L, and down R across a double pipe culvert that feeds a pond full of standing dead trees at 2.0 mi. Another flooded wood is immediately on the R, as the road, becoming narrower, winds more steeply up the mountain. It begins to bear generally S in a series of switchbacks to a lookout to the SW and the open summit at 2.8 mi. The terrific view extends from Tongue Mt. in the NE, over Lake George, and around to Crane Mt. in the W.

❋ Trail in winter: Very suitable for snowshoeing and skiing, advanced-level past the gate.

🐾 Distances: Thomas Mt. Trail (trail 64C) to pond, 1.0 mi; to gate, 1.3 mi; to culvert, 2.0 mi; to summit lookout, 2.8 mi (4.5 km). From trailhead, 3.5 mi (5.6 km). Ascent from trailhead, 756 ft (230 m). Elevation, 1956 ft (596 m).

(64E) Up Yonda Farm Environmental Education Center

Trails Illustrated Map #743: M28

THIS 73-ACRE PRESERVE and environmental education center is run by the Warren County Parks and Recreation Department. It has a small

Cat Mt. CARL HEILMAN II

museum, a maple sugaring house, perennial and butterfly gardens, year-round nature programs, and a half-dozen short trails (up to a mile long) through the woods and fields of the former farm. Trail maps and descriptions are available at the center, which can be reached by telephone at 518-644-9767 or at www.upyondafarm.com.

▶ Directions: From I-87 (the Adirondack Northway), take Exit 24 E toward Bolton Landing, and follow Co. Rte. 11 for 5.0 mi to NY 9N. Turn R (S) and travel 0.5 mi toward Bolton Landing. Up Yonda Farm is on the R across from the Candlelight Motel. From Lake George Village, take NY 9N and travel N for 9.0 mi, passing the second stoplight in Bolton Landing. Travel N 1.0 mi more; Up Yonda Farm is on the L. ◀

(65) Tongue Mt. Range Trail

Trails Illustrated Map #743: M–N29

This trail traverses the rugged backbone of the Tongue Mt. Range, which extends into the mid-section of Lake George, bounded by the shoreline of Northwest Bay on the W and the narrows of Lake George on the E. Views from open rocky sections along the trail looking to the lake and the mountains beyond are quite inspiring. The streams in the lower sections of this trail are seasonal. The trail can be quite dry for its entire length. Be sure to carry plenty of water.

This region is also home to the eastern timber rattlesnake, a threatened species in New York State. It's a treat to be able to see them in their natural habitat in one of the few places in the state where they may be found. They are not aggressive, and are seldom seen, but it's wise to take a few precautions. Wear high-top boots and use caution when approaching rocky ledges and warm sunny places. Remember, though, that rattlesnakes can be found anywhere on the mountain. It's important never to tease or corner a rattler. If you give them a wide berth and leave them alone, they'll leave you alone. Because its range and population are limited, the timber rattlesnake is protected under New York State law. It is illegal to kill, take, or possess this species without a special DEC permit.

▶ Trailhead: From I-87 (Adirondack Northway) Exit 24, drive 5.0 mi E to NY 9N. (Just before NY 9N, there are great views from the road of the Tongue Mt. Range, Lake George, and the surrounding mountains.) Driving N on NY 9N (0.0 mi), the Clay Meadow trailhead is at 4.7 mi on the R. Continue N on 9N until at 9.5 mi the N trail-head for the Tongue Mt. Range appears on the R (E). There are blue markers along this trail. ◀

FROM THE PARKING AREA along the road (0.0 mi), the trail at first heads W, somewhat parallel to NY 9N. In about 500 ft, the trail turns L, away from a tote road, and soon begins to climb. Some of this section is eroded and may be wet. At 0.6 mi, there is a jct. with the yellow-marked Deer Leap trail (66) on the L.

The trail continues climbing steadily, up and over Brown Mt., and reaches an overlook just off the trail at 1.7 mi. The forest varies from hardwoods to hemlocks as the trail reaches a small clearing at 2.0 mi. At 2.4 mi, the trail follows rock cairns across a stretch of open rock, enters the woods, and then begins climbing again across more open rock with cairns. The Tongue Mt. Camp lean-to is at 2.6 mi. There is a fine view from the lean-to area.

Past the lean-to, a couple of good views look N and W. There's much more open rock underfoot, and there are lots of blueberries in season. Cairns mark the trail.

The trail passes through some red pines, descends to a ridge, and at 3.3 mi reaches a small clearing. The trail soon climbs up and over the ledges near the top of Five Mile Mt., reaching the top at 3.5 mi. Summit elevation, 2258 ft.

From the top, the trail descends slightly and then climbs over a couple of rocky outcrops. There are occasional views to the E, S, and W. Be sure to keep in mind the rattlesnakes, and be careful where you put your hands. The trail continues its descent, passing a couple of interesting boulders along the way, reaching a stream (maybe dry) at 4.4 mi. After a couple of small level sections, and some downhill switchbacks, the trail crosses another small stream just before the intersection at the Saddle at 5.2 mi. The E/W trail is the Five Mile Point trail (68). From this point it is 1.9 mi W along the Five Mile Point trail to the Clay Meadow trailhead, and 1.7 mi E to the shoreline of Lake George.

Heading straight ahead (SW) toward Fifth Peak, the trail climbs slightly, descends into a glen, and then winds, heading E and then S again. Soon some old stonework along the trail is a reminder of the old CCC days. The trail is cut into the hill and rises steadily along a steep hillside, reaching the yellow-marked uphill spur trail for the Fifth Peak lean-to at 5.6 mi. The fairly new lean-to is about a quarter mile off the main trail. It faces away from the fabulous view as protection from the winds. There's a great view to the E, S, and W, with a view of French Point Mt. farther down the trail.

The main trail continues S, passes a steep rock face, and soon heads uphill more steeply. At 5.8 mi, it passes a small pool at the base of a cliff, and soon traverses a fairly level enclosed ridge. At 6.0 mi, it passes the site of a fire in the summer of 1985. The undergrowth has pretty well taken over again.

The trail heads downhill at a stone outcrop and soon comes to a good view of the lake and Black Mt. on the E side. French Point Mt. is to the S with First Peak farther S and to the R.

After passing a rock cairn, at 6.3 mi the trail makes a sharp L at a burned-out tree, and soon reaches a lookout with a good view of Northwest Bay. The trail soon drops sharply W and then follows downhill along a rock wall.

At 6.5 mi, there is a sign to turn R. An old unmarked trail used this col from E to W at this point. The range trail follows the sign to the R and goes uphill through hemlocks. Black Mt. is visible across the lake once again.

The trail climbs steeply again, and at 6.7 mi reaches the top of Third Peak. After crossing some open rock ledges facing S, the trail reaches a precipitous drop and then another outlook. After heading down past a L arrow with a white marker and passing a rock cairn, the trail heads into some beeches and then begins to switchback up French Point Mt., reaching the top at 7.5 mi. The summit elevation is 1739 ft. A short distance to the S on the trail there's a great view of The Narrows of Lake George, and the whole southern panorama.

The little-used trail heads S over bare rock with faint, light blue paint blazes and soon reaches another lookout. At 7.8 mi, the trail crosses open rock with ledges on the E, with some fine views. It passes a tiny pond and another S outlook, and continues following the blue-blazed rock, heading directly SW toward Northwest Bay.

At 8.0 mi, the trail descends steeply through a boulder field. After traversing toward the E, it soon turns and heads W and drops steeply to a small stream before climbing again. The trail passes through some huge oaks, comes to another lookout, then undulates up to the top of First Peak at 8.9 mi.

The trail switchbacks down the S side of First Peak through some scrubby oaks and soon comes to a grassy section with a view of the

Point of Tongue at 9.6 mi. The route passes another couple of fine views, then turns W through some junipers and at 10.0 mi goes through a narrow cleft of rock with a slanted side before leveling off for a short distance. After passing a rocky opening with a good view, the trail descends a steep pitch before climbing to a fine view to the E from the top of a flat rock.

The trail descends to another outlook and then enters the deep woods. It begins to level off and soon reaches the jct. with the Northwest Bay Trail (trail 67) at 10.8 mi. Turning L to go to the tip of the point, at 11.0 mi there's a trail jct. for the state boat dock. Turning R, the trail reaches Montcalm Point at 11.2 mi. From here it's a nice boat ride back to the "mainland," or a 5.0-mi walk back from the jct. to the Clay Meadows trailhead via the Northwest Bay Trail (trail 67).

※ Trail in winter: Novice skiing as far as the Deer Leap jct. except for one fast hill on the return; easy snowshoeing. Advanced-level skiing and moderate snowshoeing as far as Five Mile Mt. Beyond Five Mile Mt., both skiing and snowshoeing become strenuous and are best as part of a multi-day trip.

ＭＭ Distances: NY 9N trailhead to Deer Leap trail (66), 0.6 mi; to Tongue Mt. Camp lean-to, 2.6 mi; to summit of Five Mile Mt., 3.5 mi; to Five Mile Point trail (68), 5.2 mi; to cutoff for Fifth Peak lean-to, 5.6 mi; to French Point Mt., 7.5 mi; to Northwest Bay Trail (trail 67), 10.8 mi (17.2 km); to Montcalm Point, 11.2 mi (17.9 km). Elevation at trailhead, 1065 ft (325 m); Five Mile Mt., 2256 ft (688 m); Fifth Peak, 1813 ft (553 m); French Point Mt., 1756 ft (535 m); Lake George, 320 ft (97.5 m). Total trail ascent from N to S, approx. 2680 ft (817 m).

(66) Deer Leap

Trails Illustrated Map #743: N–O30

This is a short spur trail that leads from the Tongue Mt. Range Trail (trail 65) to some nice lookouts over the mid-Lake George area. There are many more spectacular views from along the Tongue Mt. trail, but the advantage of this trail is its short length. This is a fairly heavily used trail. The same cautions about rattlesnakes as described at the beginning of trail 65 pertain here, too.

▶ Trailhead: The yellow-marked trail begins at 0.6 mi S of the NY 9N trailhead for the Tongue Mt. Range Trail (trail 65). ◀

FROM THE JCT. with the Tongue Mt. Range Trail (0.0 mi), the trail heads E. After reaching an outlook at 0.3 mi, it rolls up and down over a couple of hills. After crossing an oak meadow at 0.8 mi, it arrives at a rocky opening overlooking Lake George at 1.1 mi. Here there's a view across the lake to the village of Huletts Landing on the E shore, with Sugarloaf Mt. above it and Black Mt. looming to its R.

❄ Trail in winter: Excellent snowshoeing; several narrow, twisty hills make deep snow a must for advanced skiers.

🐾 Distance: Trail 65 to Deer Leap, 1.1 mi (1.8 km). Elevation of Deer Leap, approx. 1100 ft (335 m).

(67) Northwest Bay Trail from Clay Meadow

Trails Illustrated Map #743: M–N29

This is an extremely pleasant section of trail that is not used much. It often borders the lake and was originally built as a horse trail by the CCC, but that plan was abandoned once rattlesnakes were discovered. Please read the caution regarding rattlesnakes at the beginning of trail 65.

▶ Trailhead: From I-87 (Adirondack Northway) Exit 24, drive 5.0 mi E to NY 9N. The steep hill down to NY 9N gives a good view of the undulating ridgeline of Tongue Mt. to the NE. Drive 4.7 mi N on NY 9N to a parking area on the R at an old quarry. (When this lot is full, you may find additional parking space a short distance N on the R.) About 100 ft (S) downhill along the road is the Clay Meadow trailhead for Tongue Mt., with a register. The trail is marked with blue markers. ◀

FROM THE REGISTER (0.0 mi), the trail goes downhill through a grove of white pines planted by the CCC in the 1930s. It crosses a long plank bridge over a stream at 0.2 mi, alongside a beaver dam. At 0.4 mi, it reaches a jct. Straight ahead is the Five Mile Point trail (68) to The Saddle, Fifth Peak Lean-to, the Ridge Trail and Five Mile Mt. Point on the E side of the mountain. The Northwest Bay Trail to Point of Tongue is to the R.

At 0.5 mi, the trail crosses a bridge over a stream with moss-covered rocks. At 0.7 mi, it begins to go up gradually, crossing a stream on stones, then heads uphill and into a hemlock grove alongside another picturesque stream, which it crosses. The trail becomes steeper and washed out at 0.9 mi. It reaches the top of the steep pitch at 1.1 mi, then goes downhill and crosses a plank bridge over another beautiful stream. At 1.5 mi, it goes downhill through a deeply shaded hemlock glen.

At 1.7 mi, the trail reaches the marshy head of Northwest Bay. At 1.8 mi, it crosses a stream on another plank bridge. Then it goes up alongside a hill by the shoreline under large hemlocks with a fantastic mossy cliff on the L. At 2.0 mi, a spur trail R goes 200 ft to Bear Point, where there is a nice view into Northwest Bay and down Lake George. At 2.1 mi, the trail reaches a high bluff where people have camped. Then it comes downhill and crosses another stream on a bridge at 2.2 mi.

At 2.4 mi, the trail passes a point with a fire circle. At 2.5 mi, it crosses a dry stony brook, then climbs steeply up and then down along a mossy cliff, crossing a bridge. It reaches a small point with a fire circle at 2.6 mi, then goes uphill and under hemlocks, almost level with the lake shore. This is a beautiful stretch of trail, close to the water.

At 2.7 mi, there is a nice rock to swim from. At 3.1 mi, the trail reaches an opening along the shore with a fire circle. This is also a good place for swimming. At 3.2 mi, it crosses on a log over a stream which cascades 12 ft down huge mossy blocks of rock.

At 3.4 mi, the trail crosses another stream on rocks. At 4.0 mi, it goes uphill, then down steeply to cross a muddy stream and then through a large wet area. At 4.2 mi, it descends a hill and crosses a seasonally dry brook.

The very narrow trail goes along a steep hillside just above the shore. At 4.5 mi, the trail cuts away from the clear lake and goes steeply uphill among jumbled rocks. Then it comes down steeply at 4.7 mi. At 4.8 mi, there is an opening on the shore. At 4.9 mi, the trail crosses a small stream.

At 5.0 mi, the trail reaches a jct. with the Tongue Mt. Range Trail (trail 65). To the L, French Point Mt. is 2.9 mi, Fifth Peak Lean-to is 6.2 mi, and the Tongue Mt. trailhead is 11.4 mi. Point of Tongue is straight ahead.

At 5.2 mi, the trail divides. A state dock is about 80 yd to the L on the E side of the point. There is a lovely view of The Narrows from here, as well as islands and Black Mt. and Shelving Rock Mt. (see Southeastern Lake George Wild Forest Section). S is Dome Island (a bird sanctuary owned by The Nature Conservancy), and SW is the elegant Sagamore Hotel on Green Island. Point of Tongue is a good place for a picnic and a swim at 5.4 mi (8.6 km).

❋ Trail in winter: Mostly wide and smooth, for easy and delightful snowshoeing. Intermediate skiers will be challenged only by a few fast, twisty hills.

🏃 Distances: Clay Meadow trailhead to Five Mile Point trail (68), 0.4 mi; to Bear Point, 2.0 mi; to log bridge, 3.2 mi; to Tongue Mt. Range Trail, 5.0 mi; to state dock, 5.2 mi; to Point of Tongue, 5.4 mi (8.6 km).

(68) **Five Mile Point**

Trails Illustrated Map #743: N29

This is a pretty, little-used route that connects with the Tongue Mt. Range Trail (trail 65) for reasonable-length climbs of Five Mile Mt. and French Point Mt. It then continues down the E side of the Tongue Mt. Range to the shoreline of Lake George. This is a great place to swim on a hot summer day. There are many wildflowers along the trail, and blueberries in season (around open rocky sections). Please read the caution about rattlesnakes at the beginning of the description of trail 65.

▶ Trailhead: The start is at a jct. with the Northwest Bay Trail (trail 67) 0.4 mi E of the Clay Meadow trailhead. The trail has red markers. ◀

FROM THE JCT. (0.0 mi), the trail heads directly uphill. In a short distance, a side trail branches R to a pretty waterfall that drops more than 100 ft over a series of boulders and ledges.

Continuing up, after crossing a stream at 0.3 mi, the trail becomes steep again. The trail crosses and then recrosses a stream on a couple of plank bridges, and at 0.9 mi begins a series of switchbacks up a steep and rocky hemlock-covered hill.

The trail reaches a plateau at 1.0 mi, but turns abruptly uphill again at 1.2 mi. At 1.3 mi, the grade moderates along the brook, still on the L. After a level along a moss-covered cliff with overhanging polypody ferns, there's yet another switchback before The Saddle intersection at 1.6 mi, 1180 ft above Lake George. The N-S trail is the Tongue Mt. Range Trail (trail 65). Five Mile Mt. is 1.7 mi to the L (N), and French Point Mt. 2.4 mi to the R (S).

Continuing straight ahead across the intersection, the trail is fairly level, passing a marshy section at 1.7 mi by hugging the R shoreline. The trail soon turns R and begins descending, leveling off briefly at 2.5

mi. It swings N, passes a small brook, and then turns S again.

Descending through a grassy area, there are views to Black Mt., Mother Bunch Islands, and Huletts Landing, with another lookout at 2.6 mi, just off the trail. The trail now descends through shrub oaks, junipers, and some cedars along an old horse path that was built up with some fine stonework. After a short, steep descent along some ledges and steep rock, the trail levels and enters a stand of maples and oaks. The descent is now much more gradual with lots of wildflowers along the grassy trail.

After crossing a small stream, the trail swings L and reaches Five Mile Point at 3.3 mi. The rock that descends into the lake can be nice for swimming, and makes a good landing place for a boat. Black Mt. seems to rise directly out of the water, Erebus Mt. is to the R of it, and Hatchet Island is straight ahead. To the N are the Harbor Islands, Sabbath Day Point, the cliffs of Deer Leap, and Spruce Mt.

❊ Trail in winter: The route has enough steep, twisty sections to make it a challenging snowshoe trip and an expert-level ski trip.

🐾 Distances: Northwest Bay Trail (trail 67) to Tongue Mt. Range Trail (trail 65), 1.6 mi; to Five Mile Point, 3.3 mi (5.3 km). Total distance from Clay Meadow trailhead, 3.7 mi (6.0 km).

(69) Northwest Bay Brook

Trails Illustrated Map #743: N29

This brook has some steep cascades just before it joins Northwest Bay. The short walk through a grove of pines planted by the CCC in the 1930s is pleasant.

▶ Trailhead: After parking at the quarry for the Clay Meadow trailhead (see trail 67), walk across NY 9N and downhill 100 ft to a wooden gate with a stop sign. ◀

FROM THE GATE (0.0 mi), the route goes under tall pines on a wide path, continuing 0.2 mi to the edge of a steep hill and then down about 50 ft to a waterfall on Northwest Bay Brook. Herd paths border a nice long flume below the falls; they head back E toward the highway, so a short loop is possible to and from the parking area.

🐾 Distance: NY 9N to Northwest Bay Brook, 0.2 mi (0.3 km).

(70) Charles Lathrop Pack Demonstration Forest Nature Trail

Trails Illustrated Map #743: L26

This description also appears in *Adirondack Trails: Central Region*.

This handicapped-accessible nature trail is maintained by the State University of New York College of Environmental Science and Forestry. It offers a very appealing walk of a little over a mile through one of the greatest assemblages of truly huge hemlock trees in the Adirondacks. Its most striking attraction, however, is Grandmother's Tree. Grandmother's Tree is at least 315 years old and, with a height of approximately 175 ft, is the tallest white pine tree on record in the state.

▶ Trailhead: Access is off the W side of US 9, 0.7 mi N of the US 9 and NY 28 intersection N of Warrensburg. A large sign marks the spot. Turn onto the macadam road and follow the directional signs for the nature trail parking lot. At 0.6 mi, a sign points R to parking in an unpaved open area. Returning to the main road, turn R and walk 150 yd along the road until you see the sign at L labeled "Grandmother's Tree Nature Trail." Printed trail guides are available at the trailhead. ◀

THE TRAIL ENTERS an oak-hemlock forest from the trailhead (0.0 mi). It crosses a gurgling brook on a bridge at 150 ft and the valley widens. White pine and yellow birch are now found. The trail gradually circles a glacial hill on the R. Various ferns, mosses, and lycopodia keep your interest, as the trail swings N among huge hemlocks.

The trail crosses two more bridges at 0.4 mi and 0.5 mi before reaching Grandmother's Tree at 0.6 mi. Its top soars out of sight in the forest canopy. Less than 50 yd from the tree, the trail passes the last interpretive marker and turns R on a woods road. It turns R again at a T-intersection at 0.8 mi. The winding dirt road then skirts a small pond with lily pads to a third R turn at 0.9 mi. Passing through a set of buildings on a paved road, the trail ends at the parking lot on the L at 1.1 mi.

❋ Trail in winter: This trail is very short for a winter trip, but several of the roads in this facility can be walked or skied in winter.

⚹ Distances: To Grandmother's Tree, 0.6 mi; to T-intersection, 0.8 mi; to parking lot, 1.1 mi (1.9 km).

(71) **Warren County Parks and Recreation Nature Trail**

Trails Illustrated Map #743: K26

This description also appears in *Adirondack Trails: Central Region*.

A joint venture of DEC and Warren County, the Hudson River Recreation Area provides canoe access to the Hudson River, a picnic area, and hiking/cross-country skiing trails. Users can enjoy a stay of a few hours or a day in an attractive setting of towering pines adjacent to the Hudson River.

▶ Trailhead: Access to the trailhead is off the W side of Hudson St., 2.5 mi NW of the Floyd Bennett Park stoplight in Warrensburg. The N end of Hudson St. intersects NY 28, 1.7 mi N of the NY 28 and US 9 intersection. The nature trail is 2.2 mi S from NY 28. A large nature trail–canoe access sign points the way to a parking area. There is a large wooden map at the trailhead; printed trail guides were once available, but have not been for several years. The trail once had interpretive signs along it, but many of these have disappeared and have not been replaced. ◀

THE MAP AT THE TRAILHEAD displays a number of interconnected trails that can be combined in a variety of loops ranging from 0.2 mi to 1.0 mi. The trail heading straight (W) from the trailhead reaches the Hudson River in 0.2 mi. Although most of the trails are easy to hike, a couple of short, moderate to steep pitches are encountered on the outermost loop (marked yellow on the trailhead map). The northernmost red loop (on the far R on the trailhead map) can be used to access the Hudson River, but the loop itself is overgrown (2001).

❋ Trail in winter: Many cross-country trails, some requiring considerable skill, weave through this area. While none are very long, when combined they provide a nice circuit. ◆

Summit cliffs of Sleeping Beauty Mountain. JAMES APPLEYARD

Southeastern Lake George Wild Forest Section

This region to the E of Lake George contains quite a network of trails. Bounded by the Huletts Landing area to the N and West Fort Ann on the S, this area contains a nice mix of mountains, ponds, pleasant forests, and breathtaking shoreline views. Black Mt., to the N in this section, is the highest mountain with a trail in the whole eastern Adirondack region (2646 ft).

Since this is a Wild Forest area, there is an overlapping mix of hiking trails, horse trails, and snowmobile trails. Many of the trails in this section are part of a large network of carriage paths and trails that was once part of the Knapp Estate (see below). Several of these were logging roads that were improved by the men who worked for Mr. Knapp in the early 1900s. Most were stabilized with some fine stonework and are suitable for a variety of activities. These paths and trails switchback up the mountains and form a maze of paths all through the Shelving Rock area. It's a great area for the hiker, as well as the mountain biker. At present (November 2004) there are no restrictions on mountain biking in the Wild Forest regions, except in areas with completed unit management plans. In the near future though, mountain biking will be permitted only on designated mountain biking trails in Wild Forest areas. On the SE side of Lake George, mountain bikers are permitted on all trails except those leading to the summits of Black, Buck, and Sleeping Beauty mountains.

To the NE of Shelving Rock are some lovely, little-used ponds that would be great for exploring in a small ultralight canoe. The trails quite near to Shelving Rock see intensive use, particularly on holiday weekends. You don't have to go too far away, though, to find lesser-used areas and solitude during even some of the busiest times.

At one time, the Knapp Estate, at the end of Shelving Rock Rd., consisted of 9500 acres and 75 miles of roads and trails. The people who built these roads and trails left a wonderful legacy for hiking. To learn more of the history of this area, read *Sweet Peas and a White Bridge* by Elsa Steinbeck (North Country Books, 1974), filled with anecdotes about the summer hotel visitors and staff, local characters and customs. Also of interest is *From Then Til Now* by Fred Stiles (Washington County Historical Society, 1978). The original estate house on a lower slope of Shelving Rock Mt. burned in 1917. Today the family owns about 75 acres with several camps on Pearl Point. Be sure to respect the boundaries of their land. The state owns the remainder of the land, including Black Mt., Erebus Mt., Shelving Rock Mt., Sleeping Beauty Mt., and seven ponds (all with trail access and described in this section). Hiking is possible on most of the network of roads that remains.

At this writing (2004), there is no public access through the Knapp Estate.

❋ Trails in winter: Though this area is marked for snowmobiles in the winter, there's not a lot of use, so there is some great snowshoeing, cross-country skiing, and ski-shoeing potential. Remember though, if parking near the Dacy Clearing area, that most of the trails head downhill to Lake George and have to be climbed on the way back out at the end of the day. With the exception of the mountain trails, all the trails in the region are fine for skiing, and the mountains are great snowshoe tours, especially when combined with a ski in on the more level approach routes. Specific suggestions for certain trails are included in the trail descriptions.

Suggested hikes in this region:

SHORTER HIKES:
• Inman Pond—0.8 mi (1.3 km). This is a pleasant walk on an old woods road to a picturesque pond.
• Lapland Pond—3.0 mi (4.8 km). A walk on an old woods road to a pond with a lean-to and a lot of wildlife.

MODERATE HIKES:
• Sleeping Beauty Mt. Loop—7.6 mi (11.4 km) (total round trip distance). From Dacy Clearing; great mountain views from Sleeping Beauty, and then a descent to Bumps Pond and return.
• Black Mt. from the E—5.0 mi (8.0 km) round trip. Some fine views are a good reward for this climb with some steep places up to the communications tower at the summit.

HARDER HIKE:
• Black Mt. via Shelving Rock Mt.—6.6 mi (10.6 km) one way. This

route climbs first over Shelving Rock Mt., then follows the old woods road along the Lake George shoreline, and then ascends steeply up the spectacular W route to the summit of Black Mt.

(72) **Prospect Mt.**

Trails Illustrated Map #743: I27

This trail would be best rerouted up the mountain with a more gradual rate of ascent and some switchbacks. As it is, it is a steep, rocky trail, but a fairly short climb. The current trail will only become more badly eroded as time goes on. There are no vistas along the way.

▶ Trailhead: Turn N off US 9 in Lake George village at LaRoma Restaurant. Pass three churches (the Episcopal Church has a youth hostel in summer) and then turn R onto Cooper St. Go one block, turn L onto West St., then L onto Smith St. The trail starts at the end of Cooper St., but there is no place to park there. On Smith St. there is space for about five cars at the base of the stairway leading to the trail bridge over I-87, the Adirondack Northway. ◀

THE STAIRWAY (0.0 mi) is the equivalent of about four stories of steps; it and the bridge account for 0.1 mi of hiking. On the far side, the trail markers are red. The trail goes steadily up on a wide rocky path to 0.2 mi, where it makes a gentle L and becomes more moderate. An old foundation on the R has a set of stone steps. More foundations from the inclined railway that once went up the mountain are soon passed.

At 0.3 mi, the trail resumes a fairly steady upward climb. At 0.6 mi, it crosses the toll road to the peak. After crossing the road, the trail is badly eroded. It turns R at 0.7 mi, up onto bare rock, and then makes

Buck Mt. from summit of Prospect Mt. CARL HEILMAN II

a L. At 0.8 mi, it comes to a large sloping rock wall on the R. The trail goes off to the L from this wall, then levels off until at 0.8 mi it turns R and heads uphill again. At 0.9 mi, a small stream can be heard to the L as the trail climbs steeply over bare slabs of rock.

At 1.0 mi, the trail makes a level L turn, then resumes climbing again. At 1.2 mi, it becomes even more steep, but soon moderates, then goes level through huge hemlocks and white pines. At 1.4 mi, it passes through maples and beeches as it bends S onto a ledge with a partial view E to Lake George.

The trail turns R here and arrives at the toll road at 1.5 mi, near the summit. Turn R up the road, then L into the picnic area at 1.6 mi. Uphill across the road, which has been blasted out of the summit, are the remains of the fire tower at 1.7 mi. In season there are many people on the top, including those from tour buses. The view from Prospect Mt. includes Lake George village and the lake to the E, and the mountains of Vermont off in the distance.

⚓ Distances: Smith St. to first jct. with toll road, 0.6 mi; to second jct. with toll road, 1.5 mi; to summit, 1.7 mi (2.9 km). Ascent, approx. 1600 ft (489 m). Elevation of Prospect Mt., 2041 ft (622.3 m).

PILOT KNOB PRESERVE

Trails Illustrated Map #743: J–K29

The Pilot Knob Preserve opened in 2002 after a noteworthy fundraising campaign by the Lake George Land Conservancy to reclaim its lands. The Preserve's history is unique. It was the site of a house built illegally by a fugitive drug dealer in the early 1990s; its steep hairpin driveway is rumored to have cost $1 million, paid for in cash. The notoriety of these two construction projects drew the attention of the police, and a raid ensued. Subsequent owners gladly sold to the Conservancy, the house was razed, and the only remaining structure is a summit gazebo. It is a popular destination with wide views over south Lake George and the mountains beyond.

A loop trail marked with orange disks climbs from the parking lot to the lookout and gazebo and descends along the top of the driveway and back through the woods. Visitors are asked to come down the driveway only as far as the trail turnoff at a wide R-to-L hairpin, and follow the trail back to their cars. A second trail marked with blue disks begins at the high point of the Orange Trail and zig-zags a mile to a waterfall, returning by the same route. There are numerous old paths and woods roads in the area, so be sure to follow the markers, which indicate a turn with two disks and a trail jct. with four disks.

▶ Trailhead: Take Exit 21 off I-87 (the Adirondack Northway) and turn L at the light on US 9. Turn R at NY 9L and follow it for 7.2 mi to Pilot Knob Rd. Turn L and drive 0.7 mi to the U-shaped trailhead parking lot on the R. There is a Preserve sign, a split rail fence, and a kiosk at the trailhead. ◀

(73A) Orange Trail

Trails Illustrated Map #743: J29

THE TRAIL HEADS UPHILL from the kiosk (0.0 mi) through mixed forest, bearing R and then L to cross a small sloping meadow, and arrives at a trail fork at 0.3 mi. Take the L fork up an old roadway, which steepens before the trail again bears R up into a clearing with expansive views and the gazebo at 0.5 mi.

The Orange Trail continues through the clearing S and down the gravel and asphalt driveway, to the fourth hairpin turn from the top at a wooden post and trail marker at 0.8 mi. The trail heads N across a grassy, wooded sidehill with one switchback before reaching the first fork again at 1.0 mi. It goes downhill to the parking lot at 1.3 mi.

❋ Trail in winter: Suitable for snowshoeing.

⚹ Distances: To first fork, 0.3 mi; to gazebo, 0.5 mi; to marked post on driveway, 0.8 mi; to parking lot, 1.3 mi (2.0 km).

(73B) Blue Trail

Trails Illustrated Map #743: J29

THE BLUE TRAIL leaves the clearing and old house foundation behind and to the E of the gazebo on a small gravel incline. It crosses a small boardwalk, bearing R on an old woods road through hemlock and then grassy oak meadows. It heads downhill and turns L at a fork with markers at 0.3 mi, to ascend N through a forest of pole-sized trees.

At 0.5 mi, the roadway jogs R again uphill and then down across a wet spot. Take either the L or R fork at 0.7 mi to the waterfall. The L heads uphill and bears R over a rocky ledge and down onto a washed-out roadway, reaching the top of the falls at 0.9 mi. The R fork heads slightly downhill to cross the brook below the falls at 0.8 mi and then turns L to the top of the waterfall at 0.9 mi. These last two forks form a loop and can be hiked in either direction. There are other old roads in the area, so be sure always to follow the blue markers to return to the gazebo in the clearing.

❋ Trail in winter: Suitable for snowshoeing.

⚹ Distances: Gazebo to first L turn, 0.3 mi; to R turn, 0.5 mi; to L jct. with waterfall loop, 0.7 mi; to top of falls (either fork of loop), 0.9 mi (1.5 km).

(73) Old Road on the Shoulder of Pilot Knob

Trails Illustrated Map #743: K29

Many people take a wrong turn onto this road, thinking they are heading for the Buck Mt. Trail. This old road is a lovely deep-woods walk, a connector to Lower Hogtown or the first part of a loop with return past the Buck Mt. trail jct.

▶ Trailhead: The route begins at 0.2 mi on the Buck Mt. Trail from Pilot Knob (trail 76). There are infrequent blue markers, but the road is easy enough to follow. ◀

LEAVING TRAIL 76 (0.0 mi), the road begins to go uphill beside a stream to the R. At 0.2 mi, it rounds a wide curve to the L as it cuts into the side of a hill. The stream is farther below now. At 0.3 mi, a small trail goes R down to the stream. Now the road is cut into a steep bank and the grade increases.

The road crosses a dry streambed, continuing to climb through beautiful, high, deep woods. The streambed is now down to the L. At 0.4 mi, the road crosses a wet place beneath a huge slanting rock wall on the R partially covered with mosses and ferns. At 0.6 mi, the road crests a hill with a waterfall audible ahead and below on the L.

At 0.8 mi, the road crosses a rocky, steep, damp streambed. At 1.0 mi, it meets the Butternut Brook Trail (trail 74). Uphill to the R on trail 74, it is 1.9 mi to the Inman Pond trail (75), 2.4 mi to the Lower Hogtown trailhead, making a through trip from Pilot Knob of 3.6 mi.

✳ Trail in winter: Great snowshoeing and expert skiing, downhill from E to W.

⚐ Distances: Trail 76 to top of hill, 0.6 mi; to trail 74, 1.0 mi (1.6 km).

(74) Butternut Brook Trail

Trails Illustrated Map #743: K29–30

▶ Trailhead: Drive 6.3 mi on Buttermilk Falls Rd. (trail 77) N to the Lower Hogtown trailhead on the L just before Camp Little Notch, which is marked with a "CLN" sign. There is a wide turnout for parking on the L just N of the trailhead. Perhaps this old road was used by the farmers of Hogtown, to drive their hogs and carry vegetables to Lake George for the kitchens of the boarding houses and hotels along the lake. ◀

This is a snowmobile and horse trail with only occasional blue markers. It might be a good route for cross-country skiing with a car at the Pilot Knob trailhead (see trail 73).

FROM THE PARKING AREA (0.0 mi), the road starts gradually uphill past a hillside of jumbled rock on the R at 0.2 mi. At 0.5 mi, the trail reaches a new wooden bridge over a stream. Just before the bridge an old road goes R to Inman Pond (trail 75).

The trail crosses the bridge, follows a rocky, dry streambed, then crosses another stream. Now the road goes more steeply uphill, leveling off at 0.6 mi. Here there is a side road to the R, but the trail bends

L, following snowmobile and horse trail markers. The road climbs another steep pitch to 0.7 mi, then goes downhill to the level. At 0.9 mi, the road starts uphill again, this time on solid bedrock. At 1.0 mi, an overgrown pond is visible below through the trees. The road crosses a stream, then another stream at 1.1 mi before it goes uphill again and then levels out.

At 1.4 mi, the road goes along a small ridge that appears to be an esker. Now it gently descends, coming alongside a beaver clearing and stream on the L. It crosses the stream at 1.5 mi, passing an informal path to the R, marked (2004) by blue lawn-chair strapping, then passes through a fern-filled open hardwood gully. At 1.8 mi, it crosses another stream, then goes steadily downhill following horse and snowmobile trail markers.

[At 2.4 mi, trail 73 goes L 1.0 mi over the shoulder of Pilot Knob, joining the Buck Mt. Trail from Pilot Knob (trail 76) at 3.4 mi and reaching the Pilot Knob trailhead parking lot at 3.6 mi.]

The marked trail continues downhill to 2.8 mi, where it meets the Buck Mt. Trail from Pilot Knob (trail 76). A turn to the R would take you to the summit of Buck via yellow-marked trail 76. From the jct. the trail descends 1.2 mi to the Pilot Knob trailhead parking lot, making a through trip from Lower Hogtown of 4.0 mi.

✻ Trail in winter: A nice snowshoe trip. Skiing E involves a climb and gradual descent. Skiing W involves a steep, fast descent, requiring advanced skills.

⚐ Distances: Lower Hogtown to Inman Pond trail (75), 0.5 mi; to old road on the shoulder of Pilot Knob (trail 73), 2.4 mi; to Buck Mt. Trail (trail 76), 2.8 mi (4.5 km). To Pilot Knob trailhead via trail 76, 4.0 mi (6.8 km).

(75) Inman Pond

Trails Illustrated Map #743: J–K29

▶ Trailhead: This is a truly delightful walk and pleasing to the eye. It begins at 0.5 mi on the Butternut Brook Trail (trail 74), just before a wooden bridge over a stream. ◀

FOLLOWING RED HORSE TRAIL MARKERS, the road diverges R from trail 74 (0.0 mi) and goes steeply uphill with a stream down to the L. It levels off at 0.1 mi, then curves up and L around the side of a hill through beech woods.

At 0.2 mi, a path descends to the R. It is unmarked and apparently used by off-road vehicles. The road curves L and uphill, passing a "No Camping" sign on a large hemlock as it levels and splits to fork around Inman Pond at 0.4 mi.

Bearing L, the road crosses an outlet of the pond at 0.5 mi on giant logs. The pond is visible to the R. The trail passes through a corridor lined thickly with young balsams. It goes into the woods again, crossing a rusty pipe at a wet place.

At 0.7 mi, a wooden sign with "Trail" and an arrow pointing R is nailed to a maple. Snowmobile and horse trail markers are off to the R. This little-used trail leads through hemlocks and then downhill to a small bluff at 0.8 mi, overlooking this lovely pond. There is an informal campsite here as well as an abandoned beaver house in the bog that runs down the middle of the pond to just E of this bluff.

From the fork at 0.4 mi, the R road crosses another outlet with a pipe at 0.5 mi. There is an old beaver dam above the outlet. The view down the pond is fascinating since it holds a floating bog. At 0.8 mi, the road continues straight ahead, but to the L is a fire circle above the pond edge. This is the end of the official DEC trail. The owner of lands to the N has heavily posted the boundary of the Forest Preserve and the private lands.

❊ Trail in winter: A suitable destination for skiers or snowshoers.

🐾 Distances: Trail 74 to fork near pond, 0.4 mi; to S shore bluff, 0.8 mi; to N shore fire circle, 0.8 mi (1.3 km). Lower Hogtown trailhead to either terminus, 1.3 mi (2.1 km).

(76) Buck Mt. Trail from Pilot Knob

Trails Illustrated Map #743: K29

Buck Mt. is an enjoyable climb with fine views from the open rock top on the lake side. It can be climbed from both the S (trail 76) and the N (trail 77). While the N route has less elevation gain, the more heavily used S route has a number of views along the ascent. The trail is marked with yellow markers.

▶ Trailhead: To reach the Pilot Knob trailhead, drive 4.9 mi N on NY 9L from its intersection with NY 149. Turn R at a sign for Kattskill Bay and Pilot Knob and drive 3.5 mi to the Pilot Knob trailhead for Buck Mt. on the R. ◀

From the trail register (0.0 mi), the trail heads E, passing various side paths, soon crosses a small brook, and reaches a fork at 0.2 mi. [The unmarked old road R (trail 73) goes up a low shoulder of Pilot Knob and then joins the Butternut Brook Trail (trail 74) to Lower Hogtown.]

Turning L at the fork, the trail passes through a forest of basswood, birch, white pine, oak, maple, sumac, and large grapevines. After crossing Butternut Brook at 0.4 mi, the trail turns L uphill. After another switchback, the trail climbs steeply, moderates briefly, and resumes the climb by a large boulder.

At 1.0 mi, the trail passes an old stone wall and then levels off. After crossing Butternut Brook again, the trail reaches a fork at 1.2 mi. The trail R is the Butternut Brook Trail (trail 74) to the Lower Hogtown trailhead. The yellow-marked trail to Buck Mt. heads L. The route is steep again, with views through the trees of Lake George at 1.3 mi and the N side of Pilot Knob. The trail soon switchbacks to the L and at 1.6 mi crosses a stream. It briefly levels off, crosses a small stream at 1.8 mi, and then climbs steadily through a beech woods.

Past a large tree whose roots have enveloped a boulder, steep climbing begins again at 2.2 mi. The grade eases somewhat before another steep ascent at 2.4 mi. At 2.7 mi, the trail passes a small swamp, and then at 2.9 mi climbs another steep pitch to open rock with a view. At 3.0 mi, the trail ascends steeply up solid rock. Down to the SE is Crossett Pond, the site of a Boy Scout camp.

Just before the summit, the trail descends into a col where at 3.2 mi it meets the Buck Mt. Trail from Hogtown (trail 77). The summit is to the L at 3.3 mi. This rocky peak is understandably a favorite with its excellent view of Lake George and the surrounding mountains.

❋ Trail in winter: This is a great snowshoeing trail. It's good to carry instep crampons for the steeper sections and possible ice. It is negotiable as an advanced-level ski outing, requiring at least two feet of snow.

⚹ Distances: Pilot Knob trailhead to Old Road on the Shoulder of Pilot Knob (trail 73), 0.2 mi; to Butternut Brook Trail (trail 74),1.2 mi; to summit, 3.3 mi (5.3 km). Ascent, 2000 ft (610 m). Summit elevation, 2330 ft (710 m).

(77) Buck Mt. Trail from Hogtown

Trails Illustrated Map #743: K–L29

▶ Trailhead: From the intersection of NY 9L and NY 149, drive E 1.6 mi to the intersection with Buttermilk Falls Rd. Turn L onto Buttermilk Falls Rd. In 3.2 mi, just after the jct. with Taylor Wood Rd. on the R, the road becomes Sly Pond Rd. and the pavement ends. Continuing straight ahead on Sly Pond Rd., at 8.7 mi Hogtown Rd. intersects on the R. Continue straight ahead on Shelving Rock Rd., which has a dead-end sign (this road continues on to the Knapp Estate on Lake George at 12.8 mi from NY 149). At 9.4 mi is the Hogtown trailhead and parking for the Lake George Trails System. Continue on to the L until at 9.9 mi there is a small parking lot and a sign on the L for Buck Mt. ◀

STARTING AT THE PARKING LOT (0.0 mi), the trail soon crosses a stream on stones and then starts uphill. At 0.2 mi, the trail crosses another brook in a pleasant hemlock glade. After rolling up and down for a while, the trail passes a miniature pond at 0.5 mi. At 0.9 mi, the trail crosses a stream and then at 1.0 mi another; it then goes up a steep hill, leveling off at 1.2 mi.

The trail crosses a picturesque stream with shelving rocks, another stream at 1.4 mi, and then follows along water on the L at 1.5 mi. After crossing this stream twice, the trail heads steeply uphill with the stream on the R, passing three huge boulders at 1.7 mi. Now the trail is in a mature stand of hardwoods, and closely follows the stream up a steep pitch at 1.8 mi.

At 2.0 mi, the trail goes through a narrow pass of jumbled boulders and a mossy cliff with a stream cascading through its cleft. After a wet spell, water drips from the moss-covered rock. The trail soon narrows on a gentle grade overlooking the stream. At 2.1 mi, it becomes steep again, and crosses and recrosses the stream. Shortly the trail passes between two walls of boulders, levels out, and arrives at 2.2 mi at a jct. with the Buck Mt. Trail from Pilot Knob (trail 76), which continues down to the Butternut Brook Trail (trail 74) and Pilot Knob. Turn R and climb over bare rock to the summit at 2.3 mi.

The view from the open areas on top is quite fine. It includes a panorama of Lake George and the southern Adirondack mountains, including Tongue Mt., Shelving Rock Mt., Sleeping Beauty, and Black Mt. It's a fine place to relax and enjoy the view.

❋ Trail in winter: Buck Mt. is a great snowshoe trip from either side.

Skiing would be suitable only on the approach to the climbing. Instep crampons are advised for poor snow conditions.

Distances: Parking lot to pond, 0.5 mi; to boulders, 1.7 mi; to Buck Mt. Trail from Pilot Knob (trail 76), 2.2 mi; to summit, 2.3 mi (3.7 km). Ascent, 1130 ft (345 m). Summit elevation, 2330 ft (710 m).

(78) Buck Mt. Connector Trail

Trails Illustrated Map #743: L29–30

This short trail connects the N trailhead of Buck Mt. with the road to Dacy Clearing. It is not often used since most people park at the Buck Mt. trailhead to climb that mountain or at the Hogtown trailhead or Dacy Clearing. However, it can serve as the start of a very lovely walk or ski trip using other connector roads, providing a loop back to this spot.

▶ Trailhead: The trail starts directly across from the N trailhead to Buck Mt. on the E side of Shelving Rock Rd., 0.5 mi NW of the Hogtown trailhead parking lot. A sign says, "Sleeping Beauty Mt., 3.4 mi.; Fishbrook Pond, 5.2 mi." Light blue horse trail markers help hikers stay on this little-used trail. ◀

THE TRAIL LEADS GENTLY DOWNHILL NE of the road, heading to a small brook, which it crosses. The trees are mostly beech, birch, and some hemlock. In October the forest floor is a brown and gold carpet. At 0.1 mi, the trail descends to a pleasant hollow with the beginnings of a tiny stream. Woodpeckers tap and chickadees cheep busily.

Now the trail climbs up out of the hollow past maple and ash. A tan DEC marker with "'67" on it is on a tree on this slope. The trail winds uphill around a small rock ledge and passes a few yellow DEC markers.

At 0.2 mi, the trail crosses a spring near an uprooted hemlock and passes a moss-covered ledge to the R. The trail continues gently uphill through beautiful woods of beech with some hemlock, oak, and ash, crossing another spring at 0.4 mi. At 0.5 mi, the trail meets the road to Dacy Clearing (trail 82), 0.5 mi from the Hogtown trailhead parking area.

Distance: Shelving Rock Rd. at Buck Mt. trailhead to road to Dacy Clearing, 0.5 mi (0.8 km).

(79) **Shelving Rock Falls Lakeshore Loop**
Shelving Rock Falls Trail (unmaintained)

Trails Illustrated Map #743: L29

This trail has a lot of variety in it. A nice way to do the trail is to park at one of the lower parking areas (see Trailhead below) and end the walk by passing Shelving Rock Falls. This route is the best way to see the falls, from a carriage pull-off near the top of the falls. An unmarked and unmaintained rugged path leads down to the bottom of the falls and then follows the gorge down to the bridge across Shelving Rock Brook.

This area is a popular place in the summer on weekends, especially holiday weekends, so it might be good to pick other times to visit. Camping in the Shelving Rock Falls area on the W side of Shelving Rock Rd. is restricted to 21 designated campsites in the level "pines" area along the road just N of the bridge over Shelving Rock Brook. Fires are permitted in existing fire rings. There is no parking after 9 PM in the parking areas along Shelving Rock Rd. near the Knapp Estate boundary (see section introduction). Parking is restricted to parking areas only; anyone parking along the road runs the risk of being towed away.

▶Trailhead: When traveling NW on Shelving Rock Rd. from the Hogtown trailhead (see trail 82), the E access to this trail is 2.5 mi from the trailhead on the L at the metal barrier gate, just before the bridge over Shelving Rock Brook. The N trailhead is 1.1 mi farther along (3.6 mi from the Hogtown trailhead) on the L side of the road, 0.1 mi before the private Knapp Estate, but the last parking is at the 3.4 mi point on the L. Five other trails (the first is back in the woods) with metal barrier gates are passed on the L when traveling from the E access to the N access. ◀

AT THE N ACCESS, the trail begins on the L (0.0 mi). There are signs that read "No Horses Permitted" and "Motorized Vehicles Prohibited Except Snowmobiles." The trail begins heading downhill to the R, swings L, and then reaches a trail along the shore of Lake George at 0.1 mi. The R leg ends at a metal gate before a private land boundary in less than 0.1 mi. The public route turns L and passes a pretty rock point with great 180-degree views from N to S on the lake. The trail closely follows the shoreline, sometimes right along it and other times a short distance inland. There are great views most of the way.

At 0.5 mi, the trail takes a sharp L away from the lake, then soon a sharp R to follow the shore again. It follows around a pretty little cove,

Shelving Rock Falls. JAMES APPLEYARD

then at 0.6 mi comes to a jct. The trail L is the main trail. (To the R a trail leads 0.1 mi to an old camping spot on the shore.) Here is a good view over to Log Bay Island and the shoreline beyond. There is good swimming off the ledges on a hot summer day.

The main trail contours around Log Bay, soon coming to a nice view S across a rocky point with the summit of Buck Mt. visible in the distance. At 0.9 mi, the trail takes a sharp L inland to follow around a wetland in Shelving Rock Bay. A R turn here leads a short distance onto a pine-covered point. Herons, beavers, and kingfisher all frequent this wetland.

At 0.9 mi there's a jct. with the West Shelving Rock Connector Trail (trail 80) straight ahead. Bear R, passing to the W side of an outhouse to continue on the main trail. In a short distance another leg of trail 80 comes in on the L.

Following along the wetland, the trail comes to Shelving Rock Brook and crosses it on a plank bridge at 1.1 mi. Just across the bridge on the L (the S side of the bridge) is the end of an unmaintained foot trail (trail 79A) from Shelving Rock Falls.

This area was used by Native Americans long before it was claimed by European settlers. Indian artifacts have been found in Shelving Rock Bay dating from 2700 BCE, including Vosburg points (named because this type was first found on the Vosburg farm near Albany). Pottery shards found here date from the Middle Woodland era, about 400 AD. Charcoal from a fireplace excavated near Harris Bay has been dated to 4200 BCE as documented by staff from the state museum in Albany.

After crossing the bridge, the trail continues along the wooded shoreline, until at 1.3 mi it takes a sharp switchback L and begins to ascend the side of the hill. (Straight ahead along the shore at this turn are an outhouse and an old campsite in about 100 ft.) This is the first of a series of switchbacks that continue up along the S side of the brook.

At 1.5 mi, the trail levels off in a forest of stately hemlocks, pines, and oaks. Staying level, the trail soon swings around to the top of the falls and a nice side lookout over the falls at 1.6 mi.

(A rugged, unmaintained foot trail leads from the L side of an old carriage pull-off to the bottom of the falls and then down the ravine to a plank bridge. **Warning:** Many have been hurt here. The dam at the top of the falls is algae-covered and slippery, and in the winter icy conditions make footing hazardous. Descending from just W of the pull-off just W of the top of the falls, this rocky path descends steeply to the base of the falls. This is a nice place to cool your feet in the water and enjoy the view of the falls. The route continues down through the rocky gorge past rushing rocky chasms and swirling pools under the dark, towering hemlocks. The route soon moderates, reaching the Loop Trail by a bridge near Shelving Rock Brook's entrance into the bay at 0.3 mi.)

Continuing E on the main trail, on the L are remnants of the old plank bridge that used to span the top of the falls. A crossing is not recommended here now. The trail follows around the edge of an old beaver pond, and then reenters the woods following the pretty brook. The trail is mostly level to its jct. with Shelving Rock Rd. by a bridge at 2.0 mi. This is the E access to the trail.

❉ Trail in winter: The trail would be a good ski from E to N (with some tight turns from the falls down to the lake shore), and fine for snowshoeing. This trail is used by snowmobiles. Extra caution is advised around the falls in winter.

❧ Distances: N trailhead to jct. with West Shelving Rock Falls Connector Trail (trail 80), 0.9 mi; to Shelving Rock Falls (top), 1.6 mi; to Shelving Rock Rd., 2.0 mi (3.2 km).

(80) West Shelving Rock Falls Connector Trails

Trails Illustrated Map #743: L29

This is a pair of trails from Shelving Rock Rd. that meet by the Buck Mt. Connector Trail (trail 78). These trails form an angular crisscross in the Shelving Rock Falls area between the brook and the dirt road. They are each rather short, and help to form a variety of shortened loops that also utilize the Shelving Rock Falls Lakeshore Loop (trail 79).

▶Trailhead: From the Shelving Rock Mt. trailhead (see trail 85), after a short distance there's an "S" turn in Shelving Rock Rd. From here it is 0.2 mi to the trailhead and parking lot on the L. In another 0.2 mi (0.4 mi from Shelving Rock Mt. trailhead) is the second entrance, also on the L with a metal barrier gate. The last parking area on the road is just 0.1 mi past this trail. ◀

STARTING AT THE FARTHEST E ENTRANCE, 0.2 mi from the Shelving Rock Mt. trailhead (0.0 mi), the trail parallels the road for a while and descends at a moderate grade. At 0.2 mi is the intersection with the other access trail from the R. From this intersection, each leg (straight

149

ahead or L) connects with the Shelving Rock Falls Loop (trail 79) in about 250 ft.

From the intersection, turning R to return to the road, the trail follows along a wetland for a distance and climbs gradually. After a switchback, the trail heads across a stream and reaches the road at 0.1 mi. The last parking area is less than 0.1 mi to the NW.

ᛗ Distance: W entrance to jct. with Shelving Rock Falls Loop and back to E trailhead, 0.3 mi (0.5 km).

(81) **East Shelving Rock Falls Connector Trails**

Trails Illustrated Map #743: L29

▶ Trailhead: From the pine knoll just past the bridge (0.0 mi), heading W on Shelving Rock Rd., is a pine grove. One entrance is to the L in the pines. A second entrance is by the gate on the L, 0.1 mi farther, and the third is 0.1 mi past the Shelving Rock Mt. trailhead (see trail 85) at the gate on the L. ◀

THE TRAIL HEADS W through the pines, soon coming to a power line. The trail follows the power line and at 0.2 mi comes to a jct. with another entrance on the R. (The entrance is a bit over 0.1 mi away to the R on a level trail.)

The main trail descends slightly and then, just before dropping into a deep gully with a stream, reaches a T jct. at 0.3 mi. To the R is another entrance from Shelving Rock Rd. (The entrance is about 200 ft away on a mostly level trail.) Turning L, the trail parallels the stream, which is down a steep bank to the R. The forest is dark with many tall and stately pines and hemlocks.

RICHARD NOWICKI

At 0.5 mi, the trail reaches the top of the falls on the N side. With the bridge out the only way to reach the other side is by wading, or attempting to cross on a washed-out old beaver dam. Crossing here is NOT recommended. The view from the falls is better from the other side on the Loop Trail (trail 79). It's a nice walk, though, when doing the loop and heading back to the car.

ᛗ Distance: Total trail distances, 0.6 mi (1.0 km).

(82) Hogtown Trailhead to Fishbrook Pond via Dacy Clearing and Bumps Pond

Trails Illustrated Map #743: L30

This trail is a major N-S route up the E side of the Shelving Rock trail system. Since many trails intersect along the way, this isn't just a trail to a destination; it's also used in part for other routes in this quadrant. Using this trail as a base, any number of trips of varying duration can be planned that take in mountains or other ponds.

▶Trailhead: From the intersection of NY 9L and NY 149, drive E 1.6 mi to the intersection with Buttermilk Falls Rd. Turn L onto Buttermilk Falls Rd. (0.0 mi). In 3.2 mi, just after the jct. with Taylor Wood Rd. on the R, the road becomes Sly Pond Rd. and the pavement ends. Continuing straight ahead on Sly Pond Rd., at 8.7 mi Hogtown Rd. intersects on the R. Continue straight ahead on Shelving Rock Rd. with the dead end sign. At 9.4 mi is the Hogtown trailhead and parking for the Lake George Trails System. Sign the register here. In dry weather it is bumpy but possible to drive 1.5 mi beyond the register to Dacy Clearing, where the foot trail actually begins. ◀

FROM THE REGISTER (0.0 mi), the trail follows the narrow road N, reaching the Buck Mt. Connector Trail (trail 78) on the L at 0.5 mi. At 0.6 mi, one leg of the Old Farm Rd. (trail 84A) branches off to the L. At 1.2 mi, the road passes through a small clearing on the R with a view up to the cliffs on Sleeping Beauty Mt. Soon the road goes through a larger clearing with hitching posts for horses and a jct. with the Shortway Trail (trail 85) on the L (W). The road bends around the foundations of the old Dacy farmhouse. (The Dacy family supplied the Knapps with vegetables and also helped keep the roads clear.)

After a bridge, the Longway Trail (trail 86) cuts off to the L. The road to Dacy Clearing goes R past an old stone dam in a stream.

At Dacy Clearing, 1.6 mi, the trail bears R past a steel gate, following yellow markers, and begins a steady climb uphill. At 2.0 mi, a stream crosses the washed-out road. The trail soon crosses another stream and then levels out.

At 2.2 mi, the Sleeping Beauty trail (83) departs R. (This is a more spectacular but longer and more strenuous route to the N end of Bumps Pond.) The trail bears L, now following red markers. It follows the road, going uphill fairly steeply with few switchbacks, over loose rock. An overlook is at 2.4 mi, and another at 2.6 mi. Buck Mt. is to the S, and Lake George to the SW. It's often possible to see ravens and hawks here.

The trail soon begins to level off, and at 2.8 mi begins a gradual descent, reaching Bumps Pond at 3.1 mi. On the L is the old stone chimney of a former hunting lodge that was part of the Knapp Estate. This is now an informal campsite.

The trail soon comes to the jct. with the Bumps Pond Spur (trail 87) on the L at 3.2 mi. The trail curves E around the N shoreline of Bumps Pond, then heads N, reaching the jct. with the N end of the Sleeping Beauty trail (83) on the R at 3.3 mi.

Continuing straight ahead (N) for Fishbrook Pond, at 3.4 mi the trail passes an old beaver dam, and soon after an old beaver pond. The road is wet for a while, then levels at 3.6 mi and is drier. The trail soon begins its descent past blowdown and a beaver pond L toward Fishbrook Pond, reaching a rusted culvert at 4.0 mi. Before long, Fishbrook Pond is visible through the trees, and at 4.2 mi there is a turn-off to a pretty point with a fireplace. A lean-to is visible on the N shore. From this point it's possible to walk around either side of the pond.

The trail L is the West Fishbrook Pond Trail (trail 82A). Heading to the R, the trail reaches the S lean-to at 4.3 mi. Just beyond is a rocky outcrop with a nice view of the pond and the lean-to.

The trail bridges the pond's outlet at 4.4 mi. Just beyond, an orange-marked snowmobile trail heads off to the R. The trail ends at a jct. with the Fishbrook Pond from Lake George trail (95) and the Lapland Pond Trail (trail 98) at 4.6 mi. The N lean-to is 0.2 mi W on trail 95. This lean-to is situated at a pretty spot on a rocky shelf that slopes into the pond. Great blue herons may be seen in the shallows at the edge of the pond, and owls can be heard through the night.

🐾 Distances: Hogtown trailhead to Dacy Clearing and Longway Trail (trail 86), 1.6 mi; to S end of Sleeping Beauty trail (83), 2.2 mi; to Bumps Pond, 3.1 mi; to N end of Sleeping Beauty trail, 3.3 mi; to Fishbrook Pond, 4.2 mi; to Fishbrook Pond from Lake George trail (95) and Lapland Pond Trail (trail 98), 4.6 mi (7.4 km).

(82A) West Fishbrook Pond Trail

Trails Illustrated Map #743: L–M30

▶ Trailhead: This trail begins at 4.2 mi on the trail from Hogtown Trailhead and Dacy Clearing (trail 82). ◀

FROM THE JCT. at the point on Fishbrook Pond (0.0 mi), take the L trail past the privy. At 0.1 mi, the trail crosses an inlet stream and at 0.5 mi it reaches another inlet. At 0.7 mi, the trail ends at the Fishbrook Pond from Lake George trail (95). Turning R (E) on trail 95, it is 0.2 mi to the lean-to on the N shore of Fishbrook Pond, and 0.4 mi to the intersection with trails 82 and 98.

⋇ Distance: Trail 82 to trail 95, 0.7 mi (1.1 km).

(83) Sleeping Beauty

Trails Illustrated Map #743: L30

With all the switchbacks on the trail to the summit, this is a moderate walk to a great destination. To return, either use the ascent route, or continue N to Bumps Pond and return via trail 82 along Bumps Pond to the Hogtown trailhead.

▶ Trailhead: The yellow-marked trail begins at 2.2 mi on the Fishbrook Pond Trail (trail 82) from the Hogtown trailhead. ◀

FROM THE TRAIL JCT. (0.0 mi), the Sleeping Beauty trail bears R and after crossing a wet area on logs climbs along the shoulder of a hill at 0.2 mi. At 0.4 mi, it passes a cliff on the L and soon switchbacks to the R. After another switchback, the trail becomes steeper and more eroded at 0.7 mi. It soon levels off for a short distance and then makes a R turn around a red pine on solid rock.

Soon there is a view through the trees, and shortly after at 1.1 mi the trail reaches a Y jct. The trail R continues to Bumps Pond. The L turn is a spur to the summit at 1.2 mi. From the top are fine views of Lake George and the SE Adirondacks. A narrow trail follows another ledge to just below the summit for an even broader expanse of view. Visible are Buck Mt. to the S, Shelving Rock Mt. to the W, and the Tongue Mt. area to the NW.

To continue on to Bumps Pond, from the Y intersection (1.1 mi) head N on the moderately-used trail. At 1.4 mi the trail enters a hemlock grove and soon dips into a wet hollow. After winding uphill through some birches and hemlocks, the trail begins its descent at 1.6 mi. At 2.1 mi, the trail crosses the outlet of Bumps Pond and climbs up a short hill to the T intersection with trail 82. From here it's 3.3 mi S on trail 82 to the Hogtown trailhead, making a total loop length from the Hogtown trailhead of 7.8 mi, including the 0.1-mi detour to the summit.

❄ Trail in winter: Suitable for snowshoeing.

🐾 Distances: Trail 82 to Y jct. near summit, 1.1 mi; to summit, 1.2 mi (1.9 km); via Y jct. to Bumps Pond, 2.1 mi (3.4 km). From Hogtown trailhead register to summit of Sleeping Beauty, 3.4 mi (5.4 km). Ascent, 1038 ft (316 m). Elevation, 2347 ft (715 m).

(84) **Old Farm Rd.**

Trails Illustrated Map #743: L29-30

This is a pleasant old carriage path that is currently used by both horses and hikers. Motorized vehicles are prohibited, except for snowmobiles in the winter. This old road flows gracefully downhill through a bouldery woods with many beech and hemlocks. While it has no real destination, it's a great connector trail for a number of loop possibilities.

▶ Trailhead: The trail begins at a barrier on Shelving Rock Rd. 1.3 mi W from the Hogtown trailhead (see trail 82). There are yellow horse trail markers to the jct. with trail 84A, then blue past it. ◀

FROM THE BARRIER at Shelving Rock Rd. (0.0 mi), the trail follows an old carriage path. It starts heading uphill, passing by some sizable oaks, a result of the moderating effect of Lake George on the local microclimate. Much rock work was done to stabilize this road many years ago. The trail continues at a moderate grade uphill and passes through a grassy clearing with huge maples and a rock pile on the L, remnants of farming days. The intersection with the East Old Farm Rd. Leg (trail 84A) is at 0.6 mi.

From the intersection, the trail heads in a northerly direction over rolling terrain. As the trail straightens out, look to the R for an old stone wall about 100 ft in the woods.

The trail continues straight for a while through pines and past a couple of old clearings. Soon the trail follows around an S-curve in a mixed hardwood forest and then continues on a long, gradual straightaway. At 1.3 mi, it reaches the intersection with the Shortway Trail (trail 85). To the L it's 1.9 mi to Shelving Rock Rd., and to the R it's 0.5 mi to Dacy Clearing.

Continue straight ahead across the intersection, soon going downhill and crossing a brook. The trail curves uphill to the L along the hill, then turns R again after cresting the hill. At 1.7 mi, the trail crosses a small stream where there are several huge old hemlocks. In a short distance, the trail ends at a jct. with the Longway Trail (trail 86) at 1.8 mi. At this point it's 1.0 mi R to Dacy Clearing and 1.2 mi L to the Shelving Rock Mt. trailhead.

⚲ Distances: Shelving Rock Rd. to jct. with trail 84A, 0.6 mi; to Shortway Trail (trail 85), 1.3 mi; to Longway Trail (trail 86), 1.8 mi (2.9 km).

(84A) East Old Farm Rd. Leg

Trails Illustrated Map #743: L29-30

▶ Trailhead: This connector from trail 82 to Old Farm Rd. (trail 84) begins 0.5 mi N of the Hogtown trailhead on trail 82. It has yellow horse trail markers. ◀

HEADING W from the Hogtown Trailhead to Fishbrook Pond trail (82) (0.0 mi), the trail crosses an old stone culvert at 0.2 mi. The path is built up with stonework along the hillside and for nearly a half mile runs almost level through the woods. Ground cedar, princess pine, ferns, and beech saplings grow in this pretty woods. The road rises and falls, generally meandering downhill. At 0.7 mi, it ends at Old Farm Rd. (trail 84).

⚲ Distance: Trail 82 to trail 84, 0.7 mi (1.1 km).

(85) Shortway Trail

Trails Illustrated Map #743: L29-30

▶ Trailhead: This old road starts from the first small clearing of the old Dacy farm (1.4 mi from the Hogtown trailhead on trail 82). Raspberries are filling in the clearing. It is quite probable this was a farm-to-market road down to boats at the lakeshore. It proceeds to the Shelving Rock Mt. trailhead, 3.0 mi W on Shelving Rock Rd. from the Hogtown trailhead, which is a good place to spot a car for a return trip to Hogtown trailhead or Dacy Clearing. The choices for backpacking and skiing are extensive. ◀

Because of frequent vandalism, there is no sign at the clearing. Yellow horse trail markers point L, while a red horse trail marker points R to Dacy Clearing.

FROM THE CLEARING (0.0 mi), walk L, downhill through the clearing into the woods. You are in for a treat. At 0.2 mi, the road reaches a lovely glen with a stream on the R and a stone fire circle on the L. Ahead is a barrier with a stop sign. Just beyond it is a bridge over the stream. This is an E branch of Shelving Rock Brook below the S slope of Sleeping Beauty Mt.

The road reaches a second bridge as the stream flows L to R, weaving its way downhill. At 0.3 mi, the road crosses a third bridge. Hobblebush flowers float gracefully over the stream in late May. Christmas fern and ostrich fern grow beneath a canopy of white birches, hemlock, beech, maple, and hophornbeam.

At 0.5 mi, the road reaches an intersection with Old Farm Rd. (trail 84). The trail L goes S, then splits W to Shelving Rock Rd. or E to Dacy Clearing Rd. A sign on the R points back the way you came, to "Dacy Clearing Short Way." Across a small culvert, a trail coming in on the R has a sign, "Dacy Clearing Long Way." Continue downhill, straight ahead.

The grade becomes steeper. At 0.7 mi, the road enters a hemlock glade. At 0.8 mi, it goes along a broad ridge with a stream gurgling at the bottom of the hill to the R. At 0.9 mi, it descends more steeply. As it bends L the stream comes into full view to the R below.

The road cuts across a hillside and then winds around the contour downhill to a sturdy wooden bridge with railings. A stream comes downhill from the L over a 50-ft expanse of moss-covered solid rock. Fringed polygala (gaywings) flower in bright pink profusion along here in late May. The small, tubular, tropical-looking flowers with dark green glossy leaves are an especially welcome sign after the long winter. Fringed polygala is on the state list of protected plants.

At 1.1 mi, a lovely gorge with an exquisite rocky chasm below is a great picnic and wading spot (after mosquito season). Just upstream 60 ft is a series of pleasant cascades.

At 1.3 mi, the road crosses a large wooden bridge. There is a jct. on the L at 1.4 mi with the Big Bridges Trail (trail 89). The road to the Shelving Rock Mt. trailhead continues straight ahead.

At 1.6 mi a trail to the R bears a sign for Mt. Erebus and Shelving Rock Mt. (trail 86). This route also leads back (E) to the large clearing at Dacy Clearing.

The road crosses another bridge, on the level, then ascends among mature hardwoods and white pines. More fringed polygala blooms in late May at 1.7 mi, near a large birch cut up along the road. One giant log is propped on two shorter ones to make a perfect bench for lunch, contemplation, nature study, or rest.

At 1.8 mi, a sign at an intersection says "Dacy Clearing 2.0 mi." Continue straight. In 100 ft is another jct. with a road on the R that continues N over Mt. Erebus (trail 88) and a narrower trail W up Shelving Rock Mt. (trail 88A).

At 1.9 mi, a small seasonal stream crosses the road. There is a water pipe on the L. At 2.0 mi, there is a culvert under the road. Now the road is a carpet of golden pine needles with brown pine cones. A stream to the L 4 ft below the road is another tributary of Shelving Rock Brook.

At 2.3 mi, at a jct. with the Shelving Rock Mt. Trail (trail 90), a sign says "Dacey Clearing 2.3 mi. [Dacy seems to be spelled with or without an "e" on various signs], Shelving Rock Mt. 1.5 mi, Black Mt. Point 4.6 mi, Shelving Rock Road .25 mi." Continue straight ahead. At 2.4 mi, the route ends at Shelving Rock Rd.

🚶 Distances: Small clearing at Dacy Clearing to trail 84, 0.5 mi; to trail 89, 1.4 mi; to Longway Trail (trail 86), 1.6 mi; to jct. with trail 88, 1.8 mi; to trail up Shelving Rock Mt. (90), 2.3 mi; to Shelving Rock Rd., 2.4 mi (4.0 km).

(86) Longway Trail

Trails Illustrated Map #743: L29–30

This is another beautiful "hidden" walk in the Shelving Rock area. Since the route is popular with horseback riders there are places (steep and wet) where horses' hooves have created considerable erosion and quagmires. Nonetheless, it is rather enjoyable to see a group of horseback riders coming through the woods.

▶ Trailhead: On the NW side of the large clearing at Dacy Clearing, a sign, "Stop—barrier ahead," and a horse trail sign indicate the start of an old road. This is 1.6 mi from the Hogtown trailhead (trail 82). Two privies are on the L. There is a stop sign on a steel barrier across the entrance to the road, barring vehicles. ◀

FROM THE BARRIER (0.0 mi), the trail heads NW, gently descending through the woods along a rock-strewn hill on the R. There are light blue horse trail markers. The trail, often filled with rocks, undulates through mixed hardwoods and crosses several very small brooks that

157

feed into Shelving Rock Brook.

At 0.5 mi, a rocky cliff appears to the R, on the S side of Sleeping Beauty Mt. Christmas fern, maidenhair fern, round-leaved hepatica, hobble bush, goldenrod, Dutchman's breeches, white aster, meadow rue, and violets combine to make this a wildflower lover's heaven for three seasons of the year.

The trail continues W underneath the sheer cliffs of Sleeping Beauty Mt. to the N. Polypody ferns look like a toupee on top of a huge boulder.

At 0.9 mi, the sky opens up above a small beaver meadow, a haven for birds. The trail crosses a small outlet stream on rocks placed there, then meanders above the little stream gurgling below. In mid-October the forest floor is a carpet of golden, brown, and red maple and beech leaves.

At 1.0 mi, at a jct. with Old Farm Rd. (trail 84), turn R onto a yellow-marked horse trail continuing W to Shelving Rock. Now the trail goes more steeply downhill. Horses' hooves have churned it into a muddy mire.

After another small stream crossing, the trail goes uphill on more solid ground. Mature beeches have fallen to the ground, allowing hundreds of beech saplings to start the race for light and life.

The trail now descends a gentle pitch above a tiny feeder stream for Shelving Rock Brook. Then it crosses the boulder-filled brook on a wooden bridge on top of an old, ambitiously constructed set of stone cribwork. Huge ash trees tower over this glen. The lovely rocky stream winds downhill on the L, now guarded by hemlocks, maple, and ash.

Yellow horse trail markers direct hikers to a short re-route closer to the stream to avoid a mire. Hikers may ignore the detours marked with surveyor's tape, but horseback riders will want to follow them.

Soon the trail heads down again on a gentle diagonal with a hill to the L. There is a side route marked with yellow horse trail markers and red surveyor's tape. The detour goes over and down a hill to intersect at 1.8 mi with an old road marked with blue horse trail markers. Three small logs have been placed across the road L. The Longway Spur trail (86A) is R. A lovely brook heads downhill to the L. This is the northernmost branch of Shelving Rock Brook, coming off Erebus Mt. With several attractive cascades here, the intersection is a good spot for a rest and picnic by the brook.

The trail heads WSW from the jct. The rushing stream gathers strength and flows noisily through a lovely little gorge down to the R, providing another nice spot to explore and rest.

The old trail winds through a dark and beautiful hemlock glen with Shelving Rock Brook merrily flowing down at a steeper angle on the R. The trail and stream flirt with each other, then finally become partners as they pass through a narrow draw. The trail is almost level, thanks to considerable rock work on the R.

The trail crosses a small feeder stream on rocks 300 ft before the intersection with the Shortway Trail (trail 85) from Dacy Clearing and Shelving Rock Mt. trailhead at 2.5 mi.

⋔ Distances: Dacy Clearing to Old Farm Rd., 1.0 mi; to Longway Spur Trail, 1.8 mi; to Shortway Trail, 2.5 mi (4.1 km).

(86A) Longway Spur

Trails Illustrated Map #743: L29–30

THIS SHORT CONNECTOR provides access from the Longway Trail (trail 86) to the Erebus Mt. Trail (trail 88). Leaving trail 86 at its 1.8-mi point (0.0 mi), it goes upstream 100 ft, then crosses the stream on rocks just above a small picturesque waterfall. It continues upstream with blue horse trail markers and the stream on the R. Then it winds around uphill to an intersection with a beautiful old road to the Erebus Mt. Trail (trail 88), marked with red horse trail markers, at 0.2 mi.

⋔ Distance: Longway Trail (trail 86) to Erebus Mt. Trail (trail 88), 0.2 mi (0.3 km).

(87) Bumps Pond Spur

Trails Illustrated Map #743: L–M30

▶ Trailhead: The S end connects with the Hogtown Trailhead to Fishbrook Pond trail (82), 3.2 mi from the Hogtown trailhead. The N end intersects the Erebus Mt. Trail (trail 88) 2.1 mi from the Shortway Trail (trail 85), and 1.3 mi from the Lake George to Fishbrook Pond trail (95). ◀

THE TRAIL BEGINS on the W shore of Bumps Pond (0.0 mi). Heading through the grasses into the woods, it begins a very gradual climb, passing by an old spring in a short distance. At 0.2 mi, the trail begins to descend along the top of a wooded ridge and then soon reaches a sharp switchback to the R and continues on a moderately steep descent. At 0.4 mi, there is a sharp L switchback, soon followed by another switchback to the R.

The descent moderates and soon levels off to a pleasant walk as the trail winds through the forest. Soon after crossing a stream on a plank bridge, it ends at the Erebus Mt. Trail (trail 88) at 0.9 mi.

❋ Trail in winter: A short, easy snowshoe or ski section sandwiched between more difficult terrain.

❧ Distance: Bumps Pond to Erebus Mt. Trail (trail 88), 0.9 mi (1.4 km).

(88) Erebus Mt. Trail

Trails Illustrated Map #743: L–M30

This trail runs in a NE direction centrally across the Shelving Rock trail system and helps connect routes from both sides of the region. In particular, it connects with the Ridge Trail (trail 92) in two spots, more easily linking the Lake George E shoreline area with the interior trail system. The trail proves a pretty hike, following the brook that drains the S side of Erebus Mt. (pronounced locally "Air-a-bus" and meaning "dark, unfriendly place close to Hell"). It shows little signs of use, by horses or by people, especially near its summit. While the trail doesn't lead directly to the top of Erebus Mt., those who enjoy a good bushwhack challenge might enjoy exploring the woods above the cliffs near the top of the mountain. When hiking this trail it is important to remember that this is designated as a horse trail and that some wet and muddy areas are not bridged or maintained as though it were a hiking trail.

▶ Trailhead: The S end begins on the Shortway Trail (trail 85) 0.6 mi E of the Shelving Rock Mt. trailhead (see trail 85) along Shelving Rock Rd. The N end is on the Fishbrook Pond from Lake George trail (95), 1.6 mi E of the Lakeside Trail to Black Mt. Point (trail 93), and 1.2 mi W of the intersection of trails 82 and 98 at the NE corner of Fishbrook Pond. This trail has red horse trail markers. ◀

THE TRAIL BEARS L from the Shortway Trail (trail 85) (0.0 mi) and heads gradually uphill. Almost immediately is the jct. with the First Ridge Spur trail (88A) on the L. The Erebus Mt. Trail continues on a constant gradual grade uphill to 0.3 mi, where it levels off briefly, then begins climbing again. The forest along most of this trail is a nice mix of maturing mixed hardwoods and conifers.

At 0.4 mi, the trail levels once again and soon reaches a jct. with the Longway Spur trail (86A) going R at 0.6 mi. It crosses a streambed (which may be dry), then at 0.7 mi crosses a stream on a wooden plank bridge.

The trail continues to climb at a gradual to moderate grade along the L bank of a pleasant stream that bubbles its way along over rocks and then rests in small pools. Before long, another jct. on the L at 1.3 mi is the Second Ridge Spur trail (88B).

The Erebus Mt. Trail soons climbs somewhat steeply up around a beautiful series of cascades on the R. After a brief respite, the trail climbs steadily once again along a series of rock ledges on the L, with another set of cascades off to the R. This area has a primeval feel to it. The trail then moderates briefly, crosses a plank bridge over a stream (that may be dry), and then at 1.5 mi crosses the main stream on some extensive rockwork.

The trail now continues up the R bank of the stream at a gradual grade uphill, soon reaching another plank bridge at 1.7 mi that recrosses the stream by a rocky and mossy cascade. After the bridge, the trail climbs steeply and then continues up on mostly gradual to moderate grades. The trail levels off after passing through some blowdown, and reaches the jct. with the Bumps Pond Spur trail (87) at 2.1 mi. Bear L here for the Erebus Mt. Trail.

The trail now is mostly level, wandering in and out of a streambed (mostly dry except after a rain) and through some wet and muddy areas. At 2.4 mi, the trail passes by a large rock face on the R and then follows the base of these cliffs for a while. It may be possible to catch a glimpse of the upper reaches of these cliffs through some openings in the leaves on the trees. The trail soon begins another moderate ascent, and at 2.7 mi reaches a plateau which is the highest point on this trail. From here, the trail drops and then climbs briefly again, with glimpses of Black Mt. to the N, before undertaking a moderately steep descent over a rocky trail to a jct. with the Fishbrook Pond from Lake George trail (95) at 3.4 mi.

❄ Trail in winter: This trail is fine for skiing up to its jct. with spur trail 88B. From there the steeper sections are more suited to snowshoeing, particularly the descent from the top of the trail down to the jct. with trail 95.

🐾 Distances: Shortway Trail to trail 86A, 0.6 mi; to trail 88B, 1.3 mi;

to trail 87, 2.1 mi; to 95, 3.4 mi (5.4 km). Ascent from Shortway Trail to highest point, approx. 1600 ft (488 m).

(88A) First Ridge Spur

Trails Illustrated Map #743: L29

This is the first connecting spur from the Erebus Mt. Trail (trail 88) to the Ridge Trail (92). It bears L about 100 ft after the Erebus Mt. Trail leaves the Shortway Trail (trail 85). The trail has yellow horse trail markers and orange snowmobile markers.

LEAVING THE EREBUS MT. TRAIL (trail 88) (0.0 mi), the trail heads across a wet area, then soon ascends along a rocky ledge. It levels off at 0.2 mi and comes to a wetland at 0.3 mi. It swings around the perimeter of the wetland, then at 0.5 mi heads W up a moderately steep ascent through a hemlock forest. The trail becomes more gradual for a short distance, then begins a moderate ascent up through a rocky gully with ledges on both sides. At the top of the gully it begins to level, reaching the Ridge Trail (trail 92) at 0.7 mi.

🚶 Distance: Erebus Mt. Trail (trail 88) to Ridge Trail (trail 92), 0.7 mi (1.1 km).

(88B) Second Ridge Spur

Trails Illustrated Map #743: L–M30

LEAVING THE EREBUS MT. TRAIL (trail 88) (0.0 mi) at its 1.3-mi point, this trail follows blue horse trail markers. The trail first heads W through a predominantly hemlock forest. Soon it swings to the R, then winds back and forth, climbing on gradual to moderate grades. After crossing a wet area, it meets the Ridge Trail (trail 92) at 0.3 mi.

🚶 Distance: Erebus Mt. Trail (trail 88) to Ridge Trail (trail 92), 0.3 mi (0.5 km).

(89) Big Bridges Trail

Trails Illustrated Map #743: L29

▶ Trailhead: This route, an old road, starts 2.6 mi W of the Hogtown trailhead parking area off Shelving Rock Rd., just 0.1 mi W of the bridge over Shelving Rock Brook (see trail 79). There is a V-shaped entrance to the road on the N side of Shelving Rock Rd., across from an informal camping area. A sign points E along Shelving Rock Rd. to Hogtown trailhead parking area and W along the road to Shelving Rock Mt. trailhead; however, there may not be a sign for the destination of the route heading N into the woods: it connects to the Shortway Trail to Dacy Clearing (trail 85), and to the Longway Trail (trail 86). This old road is popular with horseback riders, snowmobilers, and skiers, as well as hikers. It is marked with blue horse trail markers after a barrier with a stop sign. ◀

Past the barrier (0.0 mi), the old road goes gently uphill, then levels under tall hemlock, ash, maple, white pine, and beech. Chanterelle mushrooms may be found here in fall.

In 0.3 mi, after an almost level walk, the road crosses Shelving Rock Brook on a large wooden bridge under gigantic pines, then a smaller bridge 30 ft beyond. Now the road curves uphill above the beautiful brook below a towering cliff. Considerable rock work on the L holds the road into the hill above the brook. Another tributary cascades down the cliff before joining the brook.

The road goes more steeply uphill, continuing to follow the brook. The stream here tumbles down through a rocky ravine.

At 0.8 mi, the road crosses a wooden bridge with railings on top of a spectacular old hand-built stone abutment. This is a good place to rest and explore.

At 0.9 mi, the Big Bridges Trail meets the Shortway Trail (trail 85) between Dacy Clearing and the trailhead for Shelving Rock Mt. To the R (E) it is 1.4 mi on the Shortway Trail to the small clearing at Dacy Clearing. To the L it is 1.0 mi to Shelving Rock Rd.

⋇ Distances: Shelving Rock Rd. to bridge over Shelving Rock Brook, 0.3 mi; to Shortway Trail, 0.9 mi (1.5 km).

(90) Shelving Rock Mt. Trail

Trails Illustrated Map #743: L29

Shelving Rock Mt. is a pleasant walk with partially obstructed views from the top. There also are some nice views along the way.

▶ Trailhead: The trail starts on the Shortway Trail (trail 85) 0.2 mi from its trailhead on Shelving Rock Rd. The trail has blue horse trail markers and orange snowmobile markers. ◀

THE TRAIL DEPARTS L from Shortway Trail (trail 85) (0.0 mi) and proceeds on the level under huge white pines for 0.3 mi. It enters a hemlock glade where stonework holds the roadbed. After a couple of switchbacks, the trail moderates and heads in a more N direction. At 0.4 mi, the trail switchbacks L (W). A long, steep, rocky slope is up to the R with several walled switchbacks ahead. The trail climbs uphill over the switchbacks that get increasingly steeper, reaching the top of them at 0.7 mi.

Now the trail rolls up and down a bit and then heads downhill to a jct. at 0.9 mi. The R fork (trail 91) heads N to the Lakeside Trail (trail 93) and also leads to the Ridge Trail (trail 92). Continue straight to Shelving Rock's summit, now with yellow markers. The trail rises at an easy grade under hemlocks, swinging from N to W to S high above Lake George. At 1.1 mi, the trail makes a switchback to the L, and at 1.3 mi reaches an overlook W to Lake George and Tongue Mt.

At 1.5 mi, the trail reaches the summit, overgrown with oak and sumac. S along a narrow trail there's an overlook above the young trees in a grassy clearing. Sleeping Beauty Mt. is to the E, Buck Mt. to the S, and some of the S end of Lake George may be visible. The Knapps had a pavilion on the summit of Shelving Rock Mt. for afternoon tea parties and evening dances (see chapter introduction).

🐾 Distances: Shortway Trail to trail 91, 0.9 mi; to overlook, 1.3 mi; to summit, 1.5 mi (2.4 km). From Shortway Trail trailhead, 1.7 mi (2.7 km). Elevation, 1130 ft (344 m). Ascent, approx. 650 ft (198 m).

(91) Shelving Rock Mt. to Lakeside Trail

Trails Illustrated Map #743: L29

▶Trailhead: This interior trail connects the Shelving Rock Mt. Trail (trail 90) and the Lakeside Trail (trail 93) on the Lake George shoreline. At this writing (2004) there is no public access through the Knapp Estate at the S end of the Lakeside Trail, so the only return to Shelving Rock Rd. is by retracing one's steps back up and over the shoulder of Shelving Rock Mt., or by designing any of several long loops out of the numerous trails on the slopes and ridges of Erebus Mt. and Shelving Rock Mt. (i.e., trails 94, 92, 95, 88, 88B, 88A, 86A, 86, and/or 85; see map for these and more possibilities for even longer loops farther to the E, with the lean-tos at Fishbrook Pond as a possible overnight stop). This trail has red markers. ◀

HEADING N FROM THE JCT. (0.0 mi) with trail 90, 0.6 mi from its start on trail 85 and 0.8 mi from the Shelving Rock Rd. trailhead, the trail descends slightly, reaching a jct. in about 200 ft with a closed trail that leads to private land. The trail soon switchbacks up a ridge to the R, then heads E across the ridge. It soon turns L at a small knoll, then drops into a small col and reaches a jct. on the R at 0.3 mi with the Ridge Trail (trail 92).

The trail bears L through a notch and soon begins a steep descent. After a switchback, the trail descends steeply, moderates a bit, then gets steep again.

At 0.8 mi, the trail descends along a ravine with huge rock walls covered with polypody ferns. Still heading steeply downhill, it reaches the Lakeside Trail (trail 93) at 1.0 mi. From this jct., a L turn leads to a dead end at private land in 0.6 mi. A R turn heads N to Red Rock Bay and Black Mt. Point.

❋ Trail in winter: The upper parts of this trail are steep for skiing, particularly the descent to Lake George. They would be fine for snowshoeing, but be sure to carry instep crampons for icy conditions.

🐾 Distances: Shelving Rock Mt. Trail (trail 90) to Ridge Trail (trail 92), 0.3 mi; to Lakeside Trail, 1.0 mi (1.6 km).

(92) Ridge Trail

Trails Illustrated Map #743: L29

This route is a horse trail that follows the ridge line from Shelving Rock Mt. to the W flanks of Erebus Mt., before dropping down to the shoreline of Lake George. The rugged trail traverses mostly through deep, dense hemlock forests, but there are open hardwoods on some of the rocky ledges. The views from a couple of vistas are expansive and unique. The trail appears to be little used, by horses or people. It is maintained as a horse trail, so there are no bridges over wet areas or rock work to stabilize some of the loose areas.

A recommended hike is to head up Shelving Rock Mt. (trail 85 to trail 90), over the Ridge Trail to the Lakeside Trail (93), then S to the Red Rock Bay Trail (trail 94), and return via the Ridge Trail and the First Ridge Spur Trail (trail 88A) and back to the trailhead via the Shortway Trail (trail 85). This sounds complicated, but once on the trails it comes together easily; see the map referenced above. Total elevation gain is about 2300 ft; distance is about 10 mi over some very scenic country.

▶ Trailheads: This is an interior trail. Access is from the Shelving Rock Rd. trailhead (see trail 85) via the Shortway Trail (trail 85), the Shelving Rock Mt. Trail (trail 90), and the Shelving Rock Mt. to Lakeside Trail (trail 91). It is 1.4 mi from the trailhead on Shelving Rock Rd. to the SW start of the trail via these three trails. This access is marked with blue horse trail markers and orange snowmobile disks. The N access is from the Lakeside Trail (trail 93), 1.2 mi S of Black Mt. Point and 2.2 mi N of the jct. of the Shelving Rock Mt. to Lakeside Trail (trail 91). This access is marked with yellow horse trail markers. ◀

FROM THE JCT. at the small col with the red-marked Shelving Rock Mt. to Lakeside Trail (trail 91) (0.0 mi), the blue-marked horse trail heads E and switchbacks up a small ridge. Once on the ridge line, there is a rocky outcrop to the L from which there are some views of Northwest Bay and the Tongue Mt. area, partially obstructed by treetops.

The trail continues along the ridge, then soon takes a R turn to the ridge top. It bears L along the flat, wooded ridge top, then heads more N again. At 0.3 mi, the trail crosses the first of three wet spots in a nice hemlock forest. The trail here, as in much of the way along the top, is in a deep forest. If not for the wind blowing across the ridge it would be easy to imagine the trail following a secluded ravine.

At 0.5 mi, the trail passes to the N of a rock shelf, then soon turns L and switchbacks down into a small col, reaching a jct. at 0.8 mi with the First Ridge Spur to the Erebus Mt. Trail (trail 88A) to the R. It's 1.2 mi back to the Shelving Rock Rd. trailhead via this connector and the Shortway Trail (trail 85).

Continuing straight ahead (NE), the main trail climbs and then switchbacks up the ridge, then follows the ridge for a while. At 1.0 mi, the trail makes a sharp switchback R, heading SW along the side of the ridge. It soon swings around S and then E, and comes to some open hardwoods on top of a small cliff. First there's a view through the trees, then at 1.2 mi the trail comes to an open ledge just off the trail that's covered with lichens, caribou moss, and grasses. There are great views from the ledge that overlooks the Shelving Rock Brook basin. To the E is Sleeping Beauty Mt.; to the S is Buck Mt.; SW are Lake George and Shelving Rock Mt.; and NW is the Tongue Mt. area. Crane Mt. is in the distance beyond other mountains surrounding Lake George. Ravens often frequent this spot, floating on the thermals not far from the cliff. The trail heads up over ledges with more vistas, then heads N back into the woods. The trail is mostly level, passing a couple of wet spots, and wanders up and down through the hemlock forest. At 1.7 mi, a jct. with the Red Rock Bay Trail (trail 94) is in a wet area. A sign points L for the lakeshore, 0.8 mi; ADK's measurement showed it to be 1.4 mi instead.

Heading straight ahead (N), the main trail soon swings R (E) and then S. It winds around uphill to the ridge top heading NE, reaching a wooded rocky ridge at 2.0 mi. After one has walked in the hemlocks for so long, the open hardwoods here are like a breath of fresh air.

After following the ridge a short distance, the trail circles around a wet area, climbs over the ridge top and descends along the SE side of the ridge. At 2.2 mi is the jct. with the Second Ridge Spur Trail to the Erebus Mt. Trail (trail 88B). The snowmobile trail cuts to the R here, along with the blue-marked horse trail.

Head L for the Ridge Trail and up the rocky section that leads into a small ravine, now following yellow horse trail markers. At the head of the ravine is a sign for the trail to make a sharp L. From here the trail is mostly downhill to the lake along the NW side of the ridge. The trail descends gradually at first, then at 2.5 mi begins a moderately steep descent with The Narrows of Lake George visible through the trees on the L.

At 2.8 mi, the trail goes down around a rocky ledge where there's a sign for a vista to the L. A spur trail leads to a small cliff in about 250 ft, with superb views of The Narrows with all the islands, the Bolton Landing area, Shelving Rock Mt. and the ridge the trail has been following, Tongue Mt., and numerous mountains in the distance. The trail rolls up and down a bit, then continues its descent on gradual to moderately steep grades, with a couple of steep sections.

Soon the trail follows and crosses a couple of small streams (these may be dry in late summer). At 3.6 mi, it crosses a larger stream, levels through evergreens for a short distance, and then swings L down around a rocky outcrop. There's a sign at 3.8 mi with an arrow pointing to the R. Before long the trail comes into a section of open hardwoods, with a few huge old oak trees towering overhead. The lake is visible through the trees, and the trail descends to the Lakeside Trail (trail 93) at 3.9 mi. Just beyond to the L are a tent platform and campsite (reservations required) on a small rocky point. This is a great place to enjoy the panorama up and down Lake George.

❊ Trail in winter: Not recommended as a ski trail, but a great snow-shoe trail. With the leaves off the trees there are some better views, but not many. Instep crampons should be taken along for possible icy sections.

🐾 Distances: Shelving Rock Mt. Trail (trail 90) to First Ridge Spur Trail (trail 88A), 0.8 mi; to Red Rock Bay Trail (trail 94), 1.7 mi; to Second Ridge Spur trail (88B), 2.2 mi; to Lakeside Trail, 3.9 mi (6.2 km). Highest elevation along the trail, approx. 1550 ft (472 m).

(93) Lakeside Trail to Black Mt. Point

Trails Illustrated Map #743: L–M30

AT THIS WRITING (2004), there is no public access through the Knapp Estate (see chapter introduction). The rather involved and strenuous access to the S end of this trail is via the Shortway Trail (trail 85) from its Shelving Rock Rd. Trailhead, up the Shelving Rock Mt. Trail (trail 90), and down the Shelving Rock Mt. to Lakeside Trail (trail 91). It is also accessible by boat at one of 20 campsites along Lake George or two picnic areas, all of which have docks. Other trails also connect to this old road, providing options for hikes of various lengths: from Erebus Mt. (trails 92 and 94), from Fishbrook Pond (trail 95), and from the Pike Brook Rd. trailhead (trails 96 and 97).

Camping at one of the state campsites along the lake requires reservations, and there's a nightly fee. In winter there is good skiing along the road and also on the lake under optimal conditions. Shelving Rock Rd. is plowed in winter as far as the gate to the Knapp Estate.

This description begins at the SW end of the trail, 0.6 mi SW of its intersection with the Shelving Rock Mt. to Lakeside Trail (trail 91), which provides access from Shelving Rock Rd. as explained above, and proceeds ENE and then NE along the shoreline.

From the private land boundary (0.0 mi), the trail mostly hugs the lakeshore as it heads ENE. At 0.1 mi, there is a point on the L, and at 0.2 mi a spring by the shore on the L with a dock for boaters to obtain spring water. At 0.4 mi, the road traverses a bluff by a point looking down into a lovely cove. The jct. with the Shelving Rock Mt. to Lakeside Trail (trail 91) is at 0.6 mi. Watch Island is offshore on the L. Red trail markers are infrequent here, but that is no problem since the trail, following an old roadway, is easy to follow.

Now the road goes uphill, levels off, and then goes downhill. At 1.0 mi, it passes a lovely low point that would be a good picnic spot. Now the road is level again, passing a point that forms the S boundary of Red Rock Bay. The road descends again a short distance, coming almost level with the bay.

The road reaches Commission Point at 1.2 mi, with hemlocks, a stone picnic pavilion, grills, and picnic tables spread along the S shore with six docks on the N shore. Overnight mooring from dusk to 9 AM has a fee (although boats may dock here overnight only if the campsites are full). Dogs are prohibited. There is a view S to Shelving Rock Mt., Pearl Point, and several islands, and directly W to Fork Island and Tongue Mt. In spring and fall this is a peaceful spot with the lake empty of motorboats and the tourists absent.

The road goes uphill from Red Rock Bay, rolls up and down, then at 1.5 mi levels out by the lake. To the L there is a dock on the N side of a point. This is the first of 20 state campsites along the way. A stream goes through a culvert under the old road. To the R is a dock on the S side of a point.

At 1.6 mi the road passes a springhouse in the woods to the R. A pipe from the springhouse goes under the road, then ends in mid-air, providing a source of water.

Soon the road arrives above the second dock. There are two picnic tables, two grills, a stone fireplace, and two privies here. At 1.7 mi, there is another dock with several picnic tables, grills, a fireplace, and four privies, then two more docks.

At 1.8 mi, the road bends L. The Red Rock Bay Trail (trail 94) with yellow horse trail markers goes uphill to the R to the Ridge Trail (trail 92). Red horse trail markers indicate a little-used trail to the R. Keep on the road, which still bends L.

The road passes a R turn, then arrives at a T jct. It bears R onto a rocky bluff with a rope on a cable between two white pines above the water of Paradise Bay at 1.9 mi. The water has a green-blue tint here.

At 2.0 mi, the road meets another T jct. to complete a short loop. Turning L, at 2.1 mi the route passes an abandoned road on the R.

At 2.3 mi, the road arrives at the lake again, after an inland swing, at a tent platform, picnic table, fireplace, dock and privy. At 2.4 mi, there is a similar campsite, also with a tent platform. After a third campsite, the road goes gently uphill, passing another campsite almost out of sight on a point at 2.5 mi. At 2.6 mi, the road passes another tent platform, another campsite without a platform, a dock in a cove within 50 ft of the road, then another tent platform campsite. At 2.7 mi, the Ridge Trail (trail 92) goes R up the W side of Erebus Mt. almost directly opposite a path lined with stones to a point with a tent platform campsite. At 2.8 mi, there are two more campsites on another point, with another campsite a short way beyond.

At 3.1 mi, the trail R leads to Fishbrook Pond (trail 95). There is yet another campsite on the R, and at 3.2 mi a campsite on the lake, followed by two more campsites. At 3.3 mi, the road crosses a rock streambed (sometimes dry) and arrives at Black Mt. Point with a stone picnic shelter, many picnic tables, and privies in a grassy area. At 3.4 mi there is another picnic area on a more northern point. On the N side are five docks. The Lakeside Trail ends at 3.5 mi, where the Black Mt. Trail (trail 96) heads uphill R.

✳ Trail in winter: Excellent lake-level skiing and snowshoeing, best accessed across the lake itself, under amendable conditions.

🐾 Distances: Private land boundary at SW end to Shelving Rock Mt. to Lakeside Trail (trail 91), 0.6 mi; to Commission Point picnic area, 1.2 mi; to Red Rock Bay Trail (trail 94), 1.8 mi; to Ridge Trail (trail 92), 2.7 mi; to trail to Fishbrook Pond (trail 95), 3.1 mi; to Black Mt. Point picnic area, 3.3 mi; to trail up Black Mt. (trail 96), 3.5 mi (5.6 km).

(94) Red Rock Bay Trail

Trails Illustrated Map #743: L–M29

This trail is marked as a horse trail, but is a fine hiking trail as it switchbacks up the rugged W flank of Erebus Mt. to meet the Ridge Trail (trail 92). A nice outlook at the top of a small cliff part way up looks over the central Lake George region. The trail is sparsely marked, but not too difficult to follow. At its terminus with the Ridge Trail a DEC sign states the distance to the lake to be 0.8 mi. ADK's measurement found this instead to be 1.4 mi.

▶ Trailheads: On the N, this trail begins on the Lakeside Trail (trail 93) 1.3 mi NE of its jct. with the Shelving Rock Mt. to Lakeside Trail (trail 91), and 1.5 mi S of Black Mt. Point. The S terminus is on the Ridge Trail (trail 92), 1.7 mi from the Shelving Rock Mt. Trail (trail 90) and 3.1 mi from the Shelving Rock Mt. trailhead. The trail is marked with yellow horse trail markers. ◀

From the jct. with the Lakeside Trail (trail 93), the trail heads uphill in a SE direction, and soon switchbacks up the hillside at a gradual to moderately steep angle. At 0.2 mi, the rocky trail heads up, over and around some rocky ledges, then, after using a small streambed, heads up and L across the hill. The sparsely marked trail soon turns L and then R up through a rocky gully and then winds across a level area to the side of the hill. This is quite a rugged horse trail, parts of it being more reminiscent of High Peaks foot trails than gentle horse trails.

The trail soon begins a gradual ascent, heading S along the hillside. It becomes moderately steep along some ledges on the L, then begins a series of switchbacks, some of them fairly steep. At 0.5 mi, the trail follows along a cliff, first with views through the trees, and then with a fine panorama from a rocky ledge (50 ft from the trail) of The Narrows, Tongue Mt., and the Shelving Rock Mt. area. Just beyond this lookout is a rock knoll about 100 ft off the trail with even more expansive views.

After climbing briefly, the trail levels among some hemlocks and then wanders around and across a small stream. At a R turn the trail begins climbing up on a moderate grade. It ascends a rocky area at 0.8 mi and continues a gradual ascent, heading SW along the hillside.

The trail soon turns L at a sharp switchback, now heading NE. After more switchbacks, the trail once again heads SW on a gradual to moderate grade.

At 1.1 mi, the trail follows along a ledge on the L, on a gradual grade through a deep hemlock forest. After leveling off at 1.3 mi, the trail begins a very gradual descent to its jct. with the Ridge Trail (trail 92) at a wet area at 1.4 mi, having ascending approx. 900 ft from Lake George.

✳ Trail in winter: This is not recommended as a ski route, but would be good for snowshoeing. It would be wise to carry instep or full crampons for the potentially icy sections.

🐾 Distances: Lakeside Trail (trail 93) to lookout, 0.5 mi; to jct. with the Ridge Trail, 1.4 mi (2.2 km).

(95) Fishbrook Pond from Lake George

Trails Illustrated Map #743: M29–30

This is a nice connector trail, tying the Lakeside Trail (trail 93) with the midpoint of the trail system that runs up the E side from Hogtown to Pike Brook Rd. (principally trails 82 and 98). It climbs steadily at a fairly steep grade up along a brook that drains the N side of Erebus Mt., and contributes to several loop possibilities from both the N and the S. The trail gains about 1600 ft in elevation from the lake shore to the pond, so it's not to be taken lightly, but it adds some real diversity to the possibilities in the region.

▶ Trailhead: The W terminus is at a jct. with the Lakeside Trail (trail 93) 2.5 mi N of the Shelving Rock Mt. Trail jct. (trail 91). This is 0.2 mi S of the Black Mt. Point picnic area and 0.4 mi S of the jct. with the Black Mt. Trail (trail 93). The E end is at a jct. at the NE corner of Fishbrook Pond, 4.6 mi N of the Hogtown trailhead via trail 82 and 4.0 mi S of the Pike Brook trailhead via trails 97 and 98. The trail follows red markers and yellow horse trail markers. ◀

THERE ARE TWO BEGINNINGS to this trail where it intersects with the Lakeside Trail (trail 93) (0.0 mi). A short distance apart, these spurs join at 0.1 mi; the N leg is the official trail. The trail soon reaches switchbacks and an outlook at 0.4 mi and continues up the ravine with the stream and a steep drop-off on the L. At 0.5 mi, bear L where it looks like an old logging road might lead off to the R.

After climbing steeply along the ravine, the trail begins to moderate somewhat as it swings away from the stream. The woods are a mix of hardwood saplings interspersed with huge old trees.

At 1.6 mi, the Erebus Mt. Trail (trail 88) comes in from the R. Go straight ahead for Fishbrook Pond. The trail is now level with occasional wet spots. It passes a beautiful white ash just before reaching a ridge on the L that rises up from the N end of Fishbrook Pond. Elevation at the height of land here is approx. 1940 ft, about 1620 ft above Lake George. The trail descends moderately through an open hardwood forest, passing by a considerable amount of beaver handiwork, and at 2.2 mi meets the West Fishbrook Pond Trail (trail 82A) R. Continue straight ahead following the red markers.

At 2.6 mi, the trail reaches the N lean-to on Fishbrook Pond. This lean-to is a great place to camp or just view the pond and the wildlife from the ledge that slopes into the water in front of it. T trail continues E and at 2.8 mi with the Hogtown trail on the E side of Fishbrook Pond (trail 82) and the Lapland Pond Trail (98). The Greenland Pond trail (trail 100) is about 250 ft to the N on trail 98.

❋ Trail in winter: This is a steep trail and can be icy in spots; a great snowshoeing trail, but not a recommended ski route.

🐾 Distances: Lakeside Trail (trail 93) to Erebus Mt. Trail (trail 88), 1.6 mi; to West Fishbrook Pond Trail (trail 82A), 2.2 mi; to lean-to, 2.6 mi; to end at trails 82 and 98, 2.8 mi (4.5 km).

(96) Black Mt. Point to Black Mt.

Trails Illustrated Map #743: M30

Black Mt., on the E side of Lake George, is the highest mountain in the Lake George area. From the top of Black Mt. are some of the finest views in the Lake George region, and this trail from the shoreline of Lake George is the most spectacular way to climb to the top. It is the lesser used of the two trails up Black Mt. (the other is trail 97), but definitely the more interesting of the two. Leaving the shoreline at one of the wildest remaining areas of the lake, and then climbing past waterfalls and over open rock ledges on the way to the summit, the trail gives a feel of what it may have been like when this region was a summer home for Native Americans hundreds of years ago.

▶ Trailhead: This trail begins at the N end of the Lakeside Trail (trail 93) at Black Mt. Point, which is accessible by boat, or by one of the many trails that come from S in the Shelving Rock area. This trail is also accessible from the summit of Black Mt. via the trail from Pike Brook Rd. (trail 97). It is marked with red markers. ◀

AT THE JCT. with the Lakeside Trail (trail 93) (0.0 mi) at Black Mt. Point, the trail heads steeply uphill E. At 0.3 mi, it crosses an expanse of bedrock, moderating as it meanders through a forest of tall hemlocks. A brook down to the L comes from the Black Mt. Ponds. The trail soon crosses the brook and climbs again until at 0.6 mi it levels off briefly and bends L.

At 0.7 mi, climbing begins again, past a small gorge on the L. Then the trail bends R away from the gorge and to the E. A short detour to the gorge will bring you to a number of pretty cascades and flumes just out of sight of the trail.

At 0.8 mi, the route makes a switchback L, not far from some more rushing water. Soon the trail is back along another gorge on the stream on the L, and at 1.1 mi the cascades in the stream are once again visible from the trail.

Black Mt. JOHN KETTLEWELL

The trail soon bends R away from the stream, heading up over bare rock. At 1.3 mi, the trail climbs steeply along a huge rock filled with moss, lichens, and ferns on the L. It soon crosses a stream, then briefly levels off. At 1.6 mi, it crosses a stream on a wooden bridge, just below a small waterfall. The jct. with the Black Mt. Ponds Trail (trail 99) is at 1.8 mi; R are the Black Mt. Ponds and Lapland Pond.

Heading L, the trail climbs to 2.0 mi, where it passes a huge rock wall on the R and then comes to a rocky outcrop with a nice view. Just off the trail there's a rock ledge that overlooks the twin-like Black Mt. Ponds. The trail levels off briefly, then climbs up several switchbacks with some nice views, reaching a spur trail on the R at 2.6 mi. This trail leads to a grassy clearing and ledges with a great view to the S of Lake George and many of the islands. Below are the Black Mt. Ponds, with Lapland Pond farther E.

The main trail soon passes a slanting rock wall, then heads over bare rock and reaches the NY State Police communications tower at the summit at 2.8 mi. Here it meets the trail from Pike Brook Rd. (trail 97).

❋ Trail in winter: A great snowshoe trip with a good snowfall, or an advanced-level ski from trail 99 down to Lake George. Access is a challenge. Be sure to have instep crampons for icy conditions.

🏔 Distances: Black Mt. Point to Black Mt. Ponds Trail (trail 99), 1.8 mi; to summit, 2.8 mi (4.5 km). Elevation, 2646 ft (807 m). Ascent from Lake George, 2326 ft (709 m).

(97) Black Mt. from the East

Trails Illustrated Map #743: M30

Black Mt., on the E side of Lake George, is the highest mountain in the Lake George area. Since this trail, from Pike Brook Rd., starts at 1600 ft, it is a climb of only 1046 ft to the summit at 2646 ft. The ascent from the shoreline of Lake George on the W trail is much greater (see trail 96).

▶ Trailhead: From NY 22, approx. 18 mi S of the Fort Ticonderoga entrance road, turn W at the sign for Huletts Landing and drive 2.7 mi to a L turn onto Pike Brook Rd. At 0.8 mi is the trailhead parking lot and register for Black Mt. ◀

FROM THE PARKING LOT (0.0 mi), the route, an old road, avoids another old road to the R at 0.2 mi. Following red trail markers, at 0.5 mi the road reaches an old farmhouse and barn. It turns R here and goes up behind the farm. At 0.7 mi, the road crosses a wet place and ascends gently.

At 1.0 mi, the road reaches a jct. The Lapland Pond Trail (trail 98) to Lapland, Millman Pond, and Fishbrook Ponds (each with lean-tos) goes L; Black Mt. is straight ahead.

At 1.3 mi, the road divides; the L branch is recommended. At 1.4 mi, the trail crosses a wet place. It soon crosses a lovely brook tumbling across shelving rocks and at 1.6 mi crosses the brook at another jct., where a snowmobile trail joins the trail and veers off again. The trail goes L along the stream. It becomes steep, going up a small rock staircase. At 1.7 mi, it goes up bare rock next to the stream. Now the trail is washed out. At 2.0 mi, it follows a small streambed, then cuts R away from the stream.

At 2.1 mi, the trail becomes very steep in a fern-filled glen. At 2.2 mi, avoid a R turn for a snowmobile trail.

The trail divides again. These forks rejoin; the L fork enters a clear-

175

ing with huge open rock. Ahead are the closed ranger's cabin, tool shed, and woodshed. At 2.5 mi, the trail reaches the NY State Police communications tower. There is a view the length of Lake George, except for The Narrows, which is obstructed by the W shoulder of the mountain.

Sugarloaf Mt., directly NE, has a transmitter tower on top. Elephant Mt. to the N obstructs the view of Huletts Landing; Bluff Point is the first point in view on the E shore, with Sabbath Day Point across on the W shore. The High Peaks stretch out to the NW.

❈ Trail in winter: A good snowshoe trail with some fairly steep climbing near the top. Instep crampons are recommended for icy sections.

ᴍ Distances: Pike Brook Rd. trailhead to Lapland Pond trail (trail 98), 1.0 mi; to summit, 2.5 mi (4.3 km). Elevation, 2646 ft (807 m). Ascent, 1046 ft (337 m).

(98) Lapland Pond Trail

Trails Illustrated Map #743: M30

This is a great hiking trail that connects the Pike Brook Rd. trailhead (via the start of trail 97) and the Black Mt. area with the NE corner of the Shelving Rock trails SW of Fishbrook Pond. It also takes in three ponds (Lapland, Millman, and Fishbrook), and connects with the trails to the others in this quadrant (Black Mt. Ponds and Greenland Pond). Within this embrace are a half dozen lean-tos, all on ponds; some great hiking potential; and some great fishing, too.

▶ Trailheads: The N end of this trail is at the jct 1.0 mi SW of the Pike Brook trailhead on the Black Mt. from the East trail (97). S access is from the NE corner of Fishbrook Pond at the jct. with the trail from the Hogtown trailhead (trail 82) and the Fishbrook Pond from Lake George trail (95). ◀

FROM THE JCT. with the Black Mt. from the East trail (97) (0.0 mi), the trail heads S following blue markers. The trail goes along a wetland on the R until crossing a wooden bridge next to a beaver dam at 0.2 mi. Because of backwaters caused by industrious beavers, the routes in this area may change somewhat from time to time. At 0.5 mi, the trail passes a tiny pond, then soon crosses a stream. This section can be wet.

At 0.8 mi, the trail starts heading downhill and at 0.9 mi reaches a blue-marked spur for the Lapland Pond lean-to on the N shore. (This spur heads L over the stream and along the pond about 250 yd to a nice lean-to on a point above the pond. From the point, a giant rock slopes into the water. Ducks and herons feed in the shallows around the pond. This would be a great pond to paddle in a small ultralight canoe.)

The main trail proceeds from the jct. and at 1.0 mi crosses an inlet to Lapland Pond. After emerging from a grove of hemlocks, at 1.1 mi it meets the Black Mt. Ponds Trail (trail 99), which heads R with a sign for "Black Mt. Ponds." An informal path goes sharp L to the shore of Lapland Pond.

The trail heads L toward Millman Pond, now following yellow markers. It soon becomes a narrow, little-used footpath, crosses a couple of inlet streams, and then heads uphill at 1.2 mi, arriving at the end of a marshy section of Lapland Pond at 1.4 mi. Here the trail turns L, following the marsh, and soon crosses a brook on stones. It crosses a wet area and then heads uphill to a T jct. with a wide snowmobile trail at 1.6 mi. (The snowmobile trail L heads E and eventually comes out on lower Pike Brook Rd.) It would be good to look behind you here to note this turnoff for your return trip. Look for the trail markers, and listen for the rushing of the stream.

After turning R, the trail heads uphill with the stream on the R. It crosses the stream below a nice 4-ft waterfall. Here a snowmobile trail goes straight and the foot trail turns L.

Continuing uphill, with the stream on the R, the trail soon re-crosses the stream and goes up along the side of a hill. It comes to a flume on the outlet of Millman Pond at 1.8 mi. Soon the trail goes uphill, reaching a crest at 1.9 mi, then heads down toward Millman Pond. At 2.0 mi, the trail crosses an inlet stream on a bridge, with a bog on the L. It turns abruptly R and shortly comes to a lean-to on the E side of the pond at 2.1 mi. This is situated on a bluff that overlooks the pond. It has been very well taken care of by its adopter.

Heading S, the trail reaches the end of the pond at 2.2 mi, then turns L and uphill, following a stream and snowmobile markers. At a wet place, the snowmobile trail and the hiking trail divide. They soon rejoin after crossing a stream at 2.4 mi, and then make a sharp L.

The trail heads downhill with the stream on the L, flanked by a steep hillside. It rolls up and down a little, then climbs again and reaches the top of a pass at 2.8 mi. Now the trail heads downhill to Fishbrook Pond, crosses a stream, then turns L and keeps heading downhill, first coming to the Greenland Pond trail (100) on the L, and then, in approx. 250 ft, a jct. with the Fishbrook Pond from Lake George trail (95) to the R (W) and the trail to Hogtown trailhead via Bumps Pond and Dacy Clearing (trail 82) straight ahead. An unmaintained trail heads L (E) from this jct. There's a lean-to to the R at the N end of Fishbrook Pond, another along trail 82 at the S end of Fishbrook Pond (both of which are too close to the water, according to state regulations), and yet another 1.2 mi away on the E shore of Greenland Pond.

❋ Trail in winter: A good, challenging showshoe or intermediate-level ski trip.

❧ Distances: Black Mt. Trail to lean-to spur on Lapland Pond, 0.9 mi; to Black Mt. Ponds Trail (trail 99), 1.1 mi; to Millman Pond lean-to, 2.1 mi; to jct. with trails 82 and 95, 3.0 mi (4.8 km).

(99) Black Mt. Ponds Trail

Trails Illustrated Map #743: M30

This is a short connector trail between the Black Mt. Point to Black Mt. trail (96) and the Lapland Pond Trail (trail 98) that not only helps form some interesting loops, but is also a good trail to hike in its own right. There's a lean-to on the westerly of the two Black Mt. Ponds, and the trail passes through some nice woods and beaver work. For those who walk slowly and take the time to observe all the signs, there's the possibility of seeing a good bit of wildlife in the area.

▶ Trailheads: This is an interior trail. The W end is 1.8 mi E of Black Mt. Point and 1.0 mi S of Black Mt. summit on trail 96. The E end is at Lapland Pond on trail 98, 2.2 mi SW of the Pike Brook Rd. trailhead. The trail is marked with yellow markers. It is described from W to E. ◀

HEADING E from the Black Mt. Point to Black Mt. trail (96) (0.0 mi), at 0.2 mi the trail follows a rise with the first Black Mt. Pond below to the R, and soon reaches the edge of the pond. Across a stream and up a short, steep hill is the lean-to just off the trail at 0.3 mi. There's a nice view of the pond from the lean-to.

The trail follows along the edge of the pond, then at 0.4 mi heads up a hill and back into a hemlock woods. At 0.6 mi, it goes down a short, steep hill to an inlet to the second of the Black Mt. Ponds. It crosses another inlet at 0.7 mi and provides a view of this pond and the beaver activity there at 0.8 mi. The trail continues back in the woods,

Black Mt. Pond. JAMES APPLEYARD

reaching the jct. with the Lapland Pond Trail (trail 98) at 1.0 mi.

✻ Trail in winter: An easy winding and nearly level ski or snowshoe to two ponds.

🐎 Distances: Black Mt. Point to Black Mt. trail (96) to lean-to, 0.3 mi; to second Black Mt. Pond, 0.8 mi; to Lapland Pond Trail (trail 98), 1.0 mi (1.6 km).

(100) **Greenland Pond**

Trails Illustrated Map #743: L–M30

While this trail is short but sweet, any public route to get to it is at least 4 mi long. Greenland Pond, though, is well worth the visit. It's a pretty little pond, with a lean-to situated on the E shore, a nice place to camp and fish.

▶ Trailhead: The trail begins on the Lapland Pond Trail (trail 98) 250 ft N of the intersection of trails 82, 95, and 98 at the NE corner of Fishbrook Pond. The Hogtown trailhead is 4.6 mi to the S on trail 82, and the Pike Brook Rd. trailhead is 4.0 mi to the N via trails 97 and 98. Black Mt. Point, reachable by boat on Lake George, is 3.0 mi to the W via trails 95 and 93. The trail is marked with red markers. ◀

FROM THE LAPLAND POND TRAIL (trail 98) (0.0 mi), the trail heads E over some potentially wet areas. At 0.3 mi, it crosses a stream on stones and begins heading downhill. It soon crosses the stream again, and then turns L and continues downhill. After passing a pretty set of falls at 0.5 mi, at 0.7 mi the trail crosses another stream and then comes to Greenland Pond.

The trail follows the SW shore of the pond, crosses a couple of inlets, and then at 1.0 mi crosses a larger inlet. It continues around the S end of the pond, and crosses the outlet on a bridge. There is a jct. here; an unmarked trail S leads to private land in a short distance. The red-marked trail heads N (L) a short distance up the E shore of the pond, reaching the lean-to at 1.2 mi.

❊ Trail in winter: Good snowshoeing and intermediate-level skiing, but remote.

⚹ Distances: Lapland Pond Trail (trail 98) to falls, 0.5 mi; to Greenland Pond lean-to, 1.2 mi (1.9 km).

GULL BAY PRESERVE

Trails Illustrated Map #743: P31

This is another new project, as of 2003, for the very active Lake George Land Conservancy, and it is located just back from the NE shore of Lake George. The Preserve encompasses two short trails, a lookout over the lake, and three wetlands, one of which houses a great blue heron rookery.

▶ Trailhead: From Ticonderoga, at the intersection of Montcalm St.

and NY 22, turn R (S) on Rte. 22 for 9.5 mi to Gull Bay Rd. Turn R. At 1.8 mi, turn R (W) on to Sagamore Rd., and at 0.6 mi turn R into the parking area, which may be muddy. Park in the first clearing and then walk to the Preserve kiosk 0.1 mi up the dirt road. Please do not park in the sand pit by the kiosk; that area is being re-seeded. There are numerous woods roads in the area so keep a careful eye out for trail markers. ◀

(101) Blue Trail

Trails Illustrated Map #743: P31

THIS SHORT TRAIL leaves the sand pit behind the kiosk (0.0 mi), heading up along a rocky road. It flattens out in the woods, at 0.2 mi passes a jct. to the L with the Orange Trail (trail 102), and arrives at a lookout with wonderful views S over Lake George at 0.3 mi.

❋ Trail in winter: Very suitable for snowshoeing; the first hill could be challenging to skiers.

🐾 Distance: Kiosk to Orange Trail (trail 102), 0.2 mi; to lookout, 0.3 mi (0.5 km).

(102) Orange Trail

Trails Illustrated Map #743: P31

LEAVING THE BLUE TRAIL (trail 101), the trail descends a steep, rocky road to a jct. with double orange markers in a small clearing at 0.1 mi. Turn L and follow the road over bare rocks and vernal pools.

The trail goes over a rise with a large rock face on the L at 0.5 mi and swings R past a swamp. It bears L at an unmarked fork at 0.9 mi and downhill to openings with good views of the heron rookery on the L.

The trail crosses the outlet of a pond, bearing R at a jct. at a tree with eight orange markers. It goes through a long and lovely stand of ferns to another fork. Follow the trail L at the two orange markers as it loops over a hill, down along the shore of the pond and back to the jct. by the outlet at 1.5 mi.

❋ Trail in winter: Excellent for snowshoes; only the first hill would be problematic for skiers.

🐾 Distances: Blue Trail (trail 101) to first fork, 0.1 mi; to rock face, 0.5 mi; to unmarked fork L, 0.9 mi; to jct. at outlet of pond, 1.1 mi; loop back to outlet, 1.5 mi (2.4 km). ◆

Appendix I

Glossary of Terms

Bushwhack: To make one's way through natural terrain without the aid of a formal trail.

Cairn: A pile of stones to mark a summit or route.

Chimney: A steep, narrow cleft or gully in the face of a mountain, usually by which the mountain may be ascended.

Cobble: A small stony peak on the side of a mountain.

Col: A pass between two adjacent peaks or between high points of a ridgeline.

Corduroy: A road, trail, or bridge formed by logs laid side by side transversely to facilitate crossing swampy areas.

Duff: Partly decayed plant matter on the forest floor. Duff's ability to burn easily has started many forest fires.

Lean-to: A three-sided shelter with an overhanging roof on the openside.

Logging or Lumber Road: A crude road used to haul logs after lumbering.

Tote Road: A road constructed in connection with logging operations and used for hauling supplies. Often built with corduroy, many of these roads are still evident after eighty years and are often used as the routes for present-day trails.

Vernal (pool): Occurring in the spring, when snowmelt and rain create pools that disappear with drier weather.

Appendix II

State Campgrounds in the Eastern Region

Public campgrounds have been established by the DEC at many attractive spots throughout the state. Listed below, going generally N to S, are campgrounds that might be useful as bases of operations for hiking in the Eastern Region. A complete listing of all campgrounds is contained in a brochure of the New York State Forest Preserve Public Campgrounds titled *Come Back Next Summer.* This brochure is available from the DEC, 50 Wolf Rd., Albany, NY 12233.

Point Au Roche State Park, off US 9 near Beekmantown on Lake Champlain. Although there are no campsites, there is a small nature center, trails for all-season use, and other seasonal amenities.

Valcour Island, accessible by boat from the Peru Boat Launch site on US 9.

Cumberland Bay, 1 mi N of Plattsburgh on NY 314.

Ausable Point, US 9, 12 mi S of Plattsburgh.

Poke-o-Moonshine, US 9, 6 mi S of Keeseville.

Lincoln Pond, 6 mi S of Elizabethtown on Co. Rte. 7.

Sharp Bridge, US 9, 15 mi N of Schroon Lake in the Town of North Hudson.

Crown Point Reservation, on Lake Champlain off NY 9N, 8 mi N of Crown Point.

Paradox Lake, on NY 74, 2 mi E of Severance.

Putnam Pond, off NY 74, 6 mi W of Ticonderoga.

Rogers Rock, on Lake George off NY 9N, 4 mi N of Hague.

Eagle Point, on Schroon Lake, US 9, 2 mi N of Pottersville.

Hearthstone Point, NY 9N, 2 mi N of Lake George village.

Lake George Battleground, US 9, 0.2 mi S of Lake George village.

Luzerne, NY 9N, 8 mi SW of Lake George village.

Fishing licenses may be purchased at campgrounds or from town clerks.

For information on the islands in Lake George or on the E shore of the lake, or on Valcour Island in Lake Champlain, write for this brochure: *Island Camping*, Public Information and Publications Unit, NYS DEC, 50 Wolf Road, Albany, NY 12233.

Acknowledgments

IN REVISING THIS BOOK, I have used a number of Betsy Tisdale's and Carl Heilman's trail descriptions from the first and second editions, respectively, and want to thank them for all they did in putting together those editions. Carl, in particular, got me on my feet as I set about this project, which has wonderfully introduced me to new places and people. My huge thanks to those who have assisted with helpful information along the way. These include Mike Carr, Bill Brown, Chris Krahling, Chris Maron, Lynn Schumann, and Sarah Small of the Adirondack and Lake George Basin Conservancies; Paul Clickner, Will Geraud, Jaime Laczko, Tom Martin, Tad Norton, Jim Papero, Charlie Platt, Ed Russell, and Werner Schwab of the New York State Department of Environmental Conservation (DEC); Dr. Bill Brown, Steven Engelhart, Roger Harwood, and Gary Randorf of their own accords; Ann Bailey of ADK's Algonquin Chapter; and of course, ADK staff and mentors in this process: Neal Burdick, Jack Freeman, Tony Goodwin, Bonnie Langdon, John Kettlewell, and Andrea Masters.

About the Editors

DAVID THOMAS-TRAIN, born in Washington, D.C., has lived in Keene Valley, New York, since 1981. He has a B.A. in English Literature from Kenyon College and an M.S. in Early Childhood Education from Wheelock College. He taught in public and private early and elementary education for thirty years and has twenty years of experience leading canoeing, hiking, and ski trips in the Adirondacks, incorporating environmental education into these activities for various organizations, including the Adirondack Nature Conservancy, Adirondack Mountain Club, Adirondack Ski Touring Council, Adirondack Trail Improvement Society, and Natural History Museum of the Adirondacks. He is a co-Founder of The Friends of Poke-O-Moonshine, a grassroots organization dedicated to the restoration of the fire tower and trail on that mountain, and to its use as an environmental education site. He has been chair and/or Conservation Coordinator of the Keene Valley Chapter of the Adirondack Mountain Club for over twenty years, and a mapping consultant for the Adirondack Mountain Club and National Geographic Society map series on the Adirondacks. A volunteer for numerous Adirondack scientific and advocacy groups, he contributes his time to fund-raising, invasive species, loon surveys, and mammal tracking.

NEAL BURDICK, a native of Platts-burgh, New York, first climbed Armstrong Mt. and the Wolf Jaws with members of the Algonquin Chapter when he was fifteen years old. He began his employment with ADK as a teenage hut crew member at Johns Brook Lodge more than thirty years ago, and continues that relationship today as editor of ADK's Forest Preserve Series and editor-in-chief of *Adirondac* magazine since 1984.

In 2001 Burdick received the Eleanor F. Brown ADK Communication Award for his many contributions. His column in *Adirondac*, "Random Scoots," was described by ADK member and author David Trithart as "a masterpiece in short, apt, and often entertaining communication."

As an acknowledged expert on the Adirondacks and the New York State Forest Preserve, Burdick has written many articles for a wide variety of publications. He edited ADK's *Adirondack Reader* (third edition); *With Wilderness at Heart*, an ADK history, and *Our Wilderness*, a young people's history of the Adirondacks. He is a frequent contributor to *Adirondack Explorer* and *Adirondack Life* and he provided the Adirondacks entry in Fodor's *National Parks and Seashores of the East*. He is a member of the Steering Committee of the Adirondack Center for Writing, a commentator for North Country Public Radio, and past juror for the New York Foundation for the Arts nonfiction writing competition.

Burdick is a graduate of St. Lawrence University and at his "day job" is St. Lawrence's associate director of University Communications and university editor. He is a member of ADK's Laurentian Chapter.

Adirondack Mountain Club

Information Centers

The ADK Member Services Center in Lake George and the ADK Heart Lake Program Center near Lake Placid, at the head of the Van Hoevenberg Trail, offer ADK publications and other merchandise for sale, as well as backcountry and general Adirondack information, educational displays, outdoor equipment, and snacks.

Lodges and Campground

Adirondak Loj, on the shores of Heart Lake, offers year-round accommodations in private and family rooms, a coed bunkroom, and in cabins. It is accessible by car, and ample trailhead parking is available.

The Adirondak Loj. JAMES BULLARD

The Adirondak Loj Wilderness Campground, located on the Heart Lake property, offers thirty-four campsites, sixteen Adirondack-style lean-tos, and three tent cabins.

Johns Brook Lodge (JBL), located near Keene Valley, is a seasonal backcountry facility located in prime hiking country. It is 3.5 mi from the nearest road and is accessible only on foot. Facilities include coed bunkrooms or small family rooms. Cabins near JBL are available year-round.

Both lodges offer home-cooked meals and trail lunches.

Join Us

We are a nonprofit membership organization that brings together people with interests in recreation, conservation, and environmental education in the New York State Forest Preserve.

ADKers choose from friendly outings, for those just getting started with local chapters, to Adirondack backpacks, and international treks. Learn gradually through chapter outings or attend one of our schools, workshops, or other programs. A sampling includes:

OUR MISSION

The Adirondack Mountain Club is dedicated to the protection and responsible recreational use of the New York State Forest Preserve, and other parks, wild lands, and waters vital to our members and chapters. The Club, founded in 1922, is a member-directed organization committed to public service and stewardship. ADK employs a balanced approach to outdoor recreation, advocacy, environmental education, and natural resource conservation.

ADK encourages the involvement of all people in its mission and activities; its goal is to be a community that is comfortable, inviting, and accessible.

- Alpine Flora
- Ice Climbing
- Rock Climbing
- Basic Canoeing/Kayaking
- Cross-country Skiing and Snowshoeing

- Bicycle Touring
- Mountain Photography
- Winter Mountaineering
- Birds of the Adirondacks
- Geology of the High Peaks

Membership Benefits

- Discovery:
  ADK can broaden your horizons by introducing you to new places, people, recreational activities, and interests.
- *Adirondac* Magazine
- Member Discounts:
  20% off on guidebooks, maps, and other ADK publications; discount on lodge stays; discount on educational programs
- Satisfaction:
  Know that you're doing your part so future generations can enjoy the wilderness as you do.
- Chapter Participation:
  Experience the fun of outings and other social activities and the reward of working on trails, conservation, and education projects at the local level. You can also join as a member at large.
- Volunteer Opportunities:
  Give something back. There are many rewarding options in trail work, conservation and advocacy, and educational projects.

For more information:

ADK Member Services Center
(Exit 21 off the Northway, I-87)
814 Goggins Road, Lake George, NY 12845-4117

ADK Heart Lake Program Center
P.O. Box 867, Lake Placid, NY 12946-0867

ADK Public Affairs Office
301 Hamilton Street, Albany, NY 12210-1738

Information: 518-668-4447
Membership: 800-395-8080
Publications and merchandise: 800-395-8080
Education: 518-523-3441
Facilities' reservations: 518-523-3441
Public affairs: 518-449-3870
E-mail: adkinfo@adk.org
Web site: www.adk.org

Membership

To Join

Call 800-395-8080 (Mon.–Sat., 8:30 AM–5 PM), visit www.adk.org, or send this form with payment to:

Adirondack Mountain Club
Membership Department
814 Goggins Road
Lake George, NY 12845-4117

Check Membership Level:

o Individual $50
o Family $60*
o Student (full time, 18 and over) $40
o Senior (65 and over) $40
o Senior Family (65 and over) $50*
o Individual Life $1300
o Family Life $1950*
School _____

*Includes associate/family members
Fees subject to change.

Name _____
Address _____
City _____ State _____ Zip _____
Home Telephone ( ) _____
E-mail _____
❑ I want to join as a Chapter member*
❑ I want to join as a member at large
List spouse and children under 18 with birth dates:
Spouse _____
Child _____ Birth date _____
Child _____ Birth date _____
Bill my: ❑ MASTERCARD ❑ AMERICAN EXPRESS
          ❑ VISA   Exp. Date _____

[| | |]

Signature (required for charge)
❑ Check enclosed
* For details, call **800-395-8080** (Mon.–Sat., 8:30 AM–5 PM)

ADK is a nonprofit, tax-exempt organization. Membership fees, excluding $10 for membership benefits, are tax deductible, to the extent allowed by law.

GER

Index

Locations are indexed by proper name with Lake *or* Mountain *following.*